THE TRAINING OF ELEMENTARY SCHOOL TEACHERS IN GERMANY

BY

I. L. KANDEL

M.A. (UNIVERSITY OF MANCHESTER); PH.D. (COLUMBIA)

TEACHERS COLLEGE, COLUMBIA UNIVERSITY
CONTRIBUTIONS TO EDUCATION, NO. 31

PUBLISHED BY
Teachers College, Columbia University
NEW YORK CITY
1910

Library of Congress Cataloging in Publication Data

Kandel, Isaac Leon, 1881-1965.
   The training of elementary school teachers in
Germany.

   Reprint of the 1910 ed., issued in series: Teachers
College, Columbia University. Contributions to
education, no. 31.
   Bibliography: p.
   1. Elementary school teachers, Training of--Germany.
I. Title, II. Series: Columbia University. Teachers
College. Contributions to education, no. 31.
LB1725.G4K4 1972   372.1'1'220943   71-176926
ISBN 0-404-55031-2

Reprinted by Special Arrangement with Teachers
College Press, New York, New York

From the edition of 1910, New York
First AMS edition published in 1972
Manufactured in the United States

AMS PRESS, INC.
NEW YORK, N.Y.   10003

PREFACE

The accompanying study is an expansion of two papers presented at Teachers College, Columbia University, in the Departments of Educational Administration and Elementary Education in 1908-9. The investigations then made were supplemented in the summer of 1909 by a visit to the German Normal Schools. It was considered advisable to limit the scope of this work to the training of teachers for elementary schools, since the training of secondary school teachers presents an entirely different problem. It has so long been the practice in this country to look abroad, and particularly to Germany, for guidance in educational matters, that it is hoped that the present contribution may offer some suggestions on a question that is of vital importance for the progress of elementary education. Reference may here be made to works in this series on similar topics in France and England (Farrington, "The Public Primary School System of France, with special reference to the Training of Teachers"; and Sandiford, " The Training of Teachers in England and Wales ").

Acknowledgments are due to the Commissioner of Education and The English Board of Education for securing permits which enabled me to pursue my investigations in Germany; to the directors and instructors in the normal schools which I visited, for the ready and friendly spirit in which they gave me information; to Professors Sachs, Monroe, Snedden and Strayer, of Teachers College, Columbia University, for reading the work and offering some valuable and helpful suggestions.

I. L. K.

CONTENTS

CHAPTER I

HISTORICAL DEVELOPMENT

CHAPTER II

ADMINISTRATIVE AUTHORITIES

CHAPTER III

PREPARATORY TRAINING OF TEACHERS

CHAPTER IV

THE NORMAL SCHOOLS (VOLKSSCHULLEHRERSEMINARIEN)

PAGE

CHAPTER X

APPENDIX

THE TRAINING OF ELEMENTARY SCHOOL TEACHERS IN GERMANY

CHAPTER I

HISTORICAL DEVELOPMENT

It is a commonplace of the history of education that the educational system of a nation is the outward expression of its aims and aspirations, its traditions and its hopes. Nowhere is this more clearly exemplified than in the history of the training of teachers for the elementary schools of Germany. With a national ideal that is explicitly defined the Germans have evolved a clearly formulated system of training teachers to achieve that ideal. A system such as this, it might be felt, evolved by a nation that has long been regarded as the educational leader of the world should afford lessons of value to other countries where the importance of well-trained teachers has been a matter but slowly realized.

When education meant nothing more than imparting a certain amount of knowledge to the pupil, the necessity of training teachers could hardly have arisen, for it sufficed if the teacher was but a lesson ahead of his pupil. Nor could it have been thought of so long as teaching was considered part of the duties of the clergy. A conscious recognition of the importance of the problem did not arise until the era of the great pedagogic writers of the eighteenth century. But attempts were made as early as the thirteenth century to exercise some form of control over the teachers in the writing of the vernacular schools. These schools, out of which the elementary schools were to develop, arose about the end of the twelfth century to supply the new needs which the rapidly increasing progress of the commercial towns was creating. The Latin schools could no longer serve as a preparation for the life of the business man. Hence arose the new type of schools and with them a struggle between the municipal authorities and the local *Scholasticus* or chancellor. The church not only felt that her power was being disputed, but feared that the number of pupils in the Latin schools would be diminished. The struggle often resulted in a compromise, by which the town council was permitted to make the appointment of a teacher to keep a writing-school subject, however, to the approval of the Scholasticus, and the teacher had to agree to surrender part of his school-fees to this authority.[1] Very frequently this surrender had to be made to the Rector of the local Latin school. Wherever there was a vacancy in a writing-school, there was no dearth of candidates. These were often students who had failed to do any good at the universities, sometimes they were artisans who were able to read and write; not infrequently they were men who had already had some experience in the work. The teachers, however, were constantly moving about, for the license to teach was only given from year to year and was subject to three months' notice—conditions which were satisfactory to both sides and particularly to the teacher who found that the fees did not come up to his expectations. Nor was great circumspection exercised in the appointment of a teacher, since he could easily be got rid of if he proved incapable. But the town councils had to observe one condition, namely, to protect their appointee against any competition from an unlicensed teacher.

The *Winkelschulen* (hedge or " dame " schools) were private adventure schools opened by persons without the permission of the local licensing body. Here the merest elements of reading and writing were taught. These schools enjoyed a great popularity, probably because the fees were lower than in the recognized writing-school and because (owing to the necessities of competition) the discipline was less severe. As the towns grew and the number of recognized schools increased, some organization against the unlicensed teachers was necessary and was early put into operation. This organization took the form of a guild. The earliest teachers' guild in Germany is found in Munich as late as 1595. That this guild was a protective organization is certain, but it is not quite clear why it appears at a time when the guild system generally was nearing the end of its development. Teachers' guilds are found at about the same time at

---

[1] See Fischer, Geschichte des Deutschen Volksschullehrerstandes, I, 9.

Frankfort, Nurenberg, Augsburg, Lübeck. They have all the features of a trades' guild. In connection with the training of teachers these organizations are of some interest but of little importance. No person who was not a "master" could keep a school for the teaching of elementary subjects. To become a "master" it was necessary to go through a period of apprenticeship, to pass an examination, to teach for several years as an assistant until a vacancy (for a master) should arise in the guild. The period of apprenticeship usually lasted six years, beginning at eighteen years of age. At the end of the period of apprenticeship the apprentice announced his intention to offer himself for examination. This took place before the representatives of the town council and the elders of the guild. The subjects of examination were arithmetic, writing, geometry, and in some cases, book-keeping. After a successful examination the apprentice became an assistant teacher. As soon as a vacancy occurred in the guild, the oldest assistant teacher became a "master" on complying with the necessary ceremonials, which included the writing of the signboard to be hung before his school. The practice here described was that which prevailed in Nurenberg and varied in other places only in some minor details. The teachers' guilds continued until the end of the eighteenth century. In Lübeck, where there were two guilds, the last did not disappear until 1818. Towards the solution of the question of the training of teachers the guilds contributed nothing. For the time they were of service in insisting on some kind of preparation, however inadequate it may have been. But in adopting the methods of a trades' guild they not only protected themselves against competitors but served to perpetuate narrowing traditions and to exclude new ideas. It is rather significant that more pride was taken in being a member of a guild than in being a schoolmaster. On the occasion of a procession at Munich the teachers' guild was offered the privilege of walking without its banners among the representatives of the professions and trades, instead of taking their places with their standards among the artisans. The Munich teachers preferred the show and glitter and remained by their banners. As protective organizations the teachers' guilds can hardly have met with the success which they expected, for at Lübeck a second guild arose to represent the interests of the teachers of reading and prayers.[2]

Outside of the towns there was hardly any attempt to give more than the necessary religious instruction. Nor did the Reformation contribute to the progress of elementary education in Germany. In spite of the great tribute which Luther[3] pays to the "industrious, pious schoolmaster" and in spite of his exhortations to the clergy on the importance of the schools, the only result of the Reformation was to fix the school as the handmaiden of the church and the teacher as the servant of the parish pastor. The duty of teaching the Catechism and of giving religious instruction, which Luther and most of the Church Ordinances of the early sixteenth century entrusted to the clergy, came to be delegated to the sexton of the church. Gradually the duties of this official were enlarged so that in the Church Ordinance of Saxony in 1580 the village schools are assigned to the sexton, who is to teach reading, writing, and church-singing.[4] The sexton came to be identified throughout Germany with the schoolmaster without contributing anything to the dignity of the latter, particularly where the pastor did not hesitate to assert his superiority. The qualifications demanded from the sexton were hardly higher than those of the teacher of the writing-schools. Reading, writing, a strong voice to lead the church singing, ability to play the organ, and later a knowledge of the rudiments of arithmetic, were generally expected from the candidates. Since the right of appointment was vested in the community, subject to the approval of the local patron or the pastor, great discrimination could not be expected. The candidates came from the same class as the writing-school teacher, and when after the Thirty Years' War crippled soldiers and veterans presented themselves as candidates for the twofold position, there was no reason to object to their appointment. To the Reformation is due the association of school-keeping with the subordinate duties of the church as well as the subjection of the teacher to the pastor, a condition of things from which the teacher is still struggling to free himself.

---

[2]On teachers' guilds see Fischer, I, ch. 8.

[3]Painter, Luther on Education, pp. 142, 143.

[4]Mertz, Das Schulwesen der deutschen Reformation, ch. 8; Fischer, I. pp. 86-101.

It is usual in Germany to trace the impulse to establish a system of training teachers to Ratke and Comenius. To do this is to miss the point emphasized by both these writers, namely, the universality of the methods, which they suggest. With them skill in teaching depends on a knowledge of their methods, which could be obtained by private study. "As soon as we have discovered the proper method," says Comenius, "it will be no harder to teach schoolboys in any number, than with the help of the printing-press to cover a thousand sheets daily with the neatest writing."[5] And elsewhere he says, "There is one factor which by its absence or its presence can render the whole organization of a school of no avail or can aid it in the highest degree, and that is a proper supply of comprehensive and methodical class-books. It is evident that the success of my scheme depends entirely on a supply of encyclopaedic class-books."[6] Nor can the system which Comenius suggests of dividing a class into decuries under the charge of a decurion be regarded as a method of training teachers so much as a class-room device. Trotzendorf (1523) had already employed this system in a form which more nearly resembled the monitorial system later introduced by Lancaster, but which was not intended to train teachers so much as to carry out completely the Roman organization on which the school at Goldberg was based.[7] Indirectly both Ratke and Comenius, in so far as they awakened an interest in educational questions, contributed to general progress and only in this sense may they be said to have shown the need of teachers with a good preparation.

To Duke Ernest the Pious[8] belongs the honor of having been the first to recognize explicitly the necessity of training teachers. Enthusiastic as he was for the educational welfare of his state, he saw clearly that it would be impossible to establish a sound educational system until properly qualified teachers could be obtained. Unfortunately for the plan the Thirty Years' War had depleted the treasury of the Duke. He accordingly embodied his proposals in his will, which he drew up in 1654. "It is very desirable," he writes, "that the teachers at their expense or with

---

[5]Comenius, Magna Didactica (Keatinge's transl., p. 248).
[6]Ibid., p. 449.
[7]Barnard, German Teachers and Educators, pp. 185-192.
[8]Schmid, Encyklopädie des gesamten Erziehungs und Unterrichtswesen, vol. 10, p. 50.

assistance remain in one central place and . . . . through practice learn that . . . . for which they will in the future be employed. Since we in our lifetime could not establish such an institution nor assign a place and means for this purpose, our heirs and successors in the future will, if with the blessing of God they obtain more means, carry out the work with the help of the state in accordance with this intent." It was not until 1698 that the means were found by his grandson, Frederick II, of Gotha. Ten *"Seminaria scholastica"* were established. Ten of the most skilled schoolmasters were summoned before the supreme consistory and ordered "that they should as *Moderatores* assist with the necessary guidance those who wished to apply themselves to schoolkeeping." The *Moderatores circulorum seminarii scholastici,* as the directors of the ten training centres were called, soon received their instructions. In addition to religious and secular subjects the candidates were to listen to the lessons given by the directors and themselves to give lessons in their presence. "After that he (the director), should discuss the *School-method* with them at certain hours and not only point out how to act in accordance with that, but honestly tell them this or that advantage which he, the preceptor, has found practicable and also to give them a model lesson in the school so that they may learn well how to apply it hereafter."[9] But this experiment was shortlived, for it was found difficult to make even the first payments to the directors which had been promised. The experiment was dropped and bore little fruit, since it was soon overshadowed by another movement out of which the whole system of training teachers in Germany was to develop.

Under the influence of the pietistic movement greater interest began to be shown in the education of the people. The difficulty of obtaining suitable teachers soon manifested itself. According to the author of *"Sieben Böse Geister,"*[10] a satire descriptive of conditions at the end of the seventeenth century, the teachers in the elementary schools were utterly incompetent and to this was added the fact that many continued to practice some handicraft even in school hours. The pietists soon began to pay

[9]Ibid.
[10]Quoted in Kreitz, Diesterweg und die Lehrerbildung, p. 9. See also Sammlung Selten Gewordenen pädagogischen Schriften des 16ten und 17ten Jahrhunderts, vol. 7.

some attention to this state of affairs and under the impulse of Francke the foundations for the normal schools of Germany were laid. In 1696 Francke established the *Seminarium praeceptorum* in connection with his institutions at Halle. In order to have candidates at hand to fill vacancies in his schools, he introduced the practice of giving free board to some 120 students on condition that they taught for two hours daily or copied out sermons for Francke and his friends. For the guidance of these students Francke drew up the *Instructions* or *School Ordinance* in full detail.[11] Points of difficulty had to be reported to the inspectors. Conferences were held, at which the work of the school was discussed. The practice of listening to the lessons of other teachers was also introduced. It was the duty of the inspector to visit the classrooms to see whether the preceptors carried out the ordinances. In addition to the *Seminarium praeceptorum* Francke also instituted a *Seminarium selectum praeceptorum* consisting of students, not more than twelve in number, who were selected from the ordinary boarders. These had a good foundation in theology and showed skill in teaching. In a course lasting two years they were prepared to teach in Latin schools on condition that they would accept an appointment in the Orphanage or the Royal Paidagogium for three years after their training. The advantages accruing to Germany generally from Francke's work were incalculable. Not only was there a supply of good teachers for the schools, but many of the theologians who later obtained preferments were in a better position to take an intelligent interest and to exercise a salutary influence on education in their parishes.

The work of Francke was taken up and carried on in other parts of Prussia by two of his pupils—J. C. Schienmeyer and J. J. Hecker.[12] The former established an orphanage in Stettin to which at the order of the king, Frederick William I, he added a department for the training of teachers in 1732. Under the same royal influence Abbot Steinmetz established a normal school at Kloster Bergen near Magdeburg, where the lackeys and servants of the young noblemen, who attended the Paidagogium, received some training. It is to be noticed that both Frederick

---

[11]Francke, Erinnerung an Studierende der Theologie.
[12]Schmid, Encykl., 10, 51-55.

William and Frederick the Great took a very keen interest in the education of the people.[13] So far as the schools under their own patronage went they honestly endeavored to introduce a better class of teacher. That they failed was not due to absence of regulations, but to the evil traditions which had been established and the inability to exercise any coercion over the noble patrons of the schools.

Of more enduring influence, however, was the normal school established by Hecker in connection with his Real school in Berlin. His attention was directed to the question by the difficulty which he experienced in obtaining suitable teachers for the lower classes of his school. He represented in an address to the king, Frederick the Great, the necessity of establishing normal schools not only in Berlin but also in other parts of the state. The normal school in Berlin was opened as a private institution in 1748. The pupils were divided into two classes, those who only came for a short course and left as soon as their means came to an end, and a selected few who received support and took a fuller and longer course. The former, who very often were artisans desiring to eke out their income by keeping school, did not have any teaching practice. The course which was offered was somewhat varied and extensive and, as it is representative of the work done in the normal schools for the next century, may here be mentioned. The greatest importance was attached to instruction in religion and singing. The secular subjects included reading, caligraphy, ciphering, German, geography, history, natural history and meteorology, a short course in pedagogy and method, and gardening, tree-culture and the breeding of the silkworm. The inclusion of the practical subjects was due to the influence of the King, who desired in this way to foster the industry of the state and indirectly to offer an additional means of support to the teachers. In 1753 the King gave the institution an annual grant and extended for the whole state the order, which he had issued in 1752 for the schools on the royal estates, to the effect that all vacancies should be filled with teachers from the Berlin normal school. But the King himself frustrated the good intentions of this decree and of the *General-Landschul-Reglement,* when in 1779 he countenanced an order which encouraged the

---

[13]Cf. the Principia Regulativa, 1736, and the General-Landschul-reglement, 1763.

employment of disabled and veteran soldiers. But general interest and enthusiasm were now aroused and from the founding of the normal school in Berlin to the end of the century scarcely a year passed without a record of the foundation of a normal school in some part of Germany. Some were founded by means of private endowment, as the normal school in Hannover (1751). Others owed their foundation to the efforts of educationalists; Halberstadt, for instance, was established on the suggestion and through the interest of Von Rochow (1778).[14]

Basedow's contribution to the question of the training of teachers scarcely deserves consideration, were it not for the fact that he is given more credit than he deserves. In the *Agatha-erator* in which he drew up a plan for a Seminar he proposes an institution where young people under an inspector might practice better methods and spread them to other normal schools. In soliciting funds for the Philanthropinum he says that the system of education must be changed and first through normal schools. The institution was opened in 1775 with a great flourish for "gentlemen commoners" (*Pensionisten*) and servitors (*Famulanten*). From among the latter, who were to be boys between the ages of eleven and fifteen, he proposed to get teachers. The best of them were to go through the same course as the commoners, and were to become tutors in good schools and houses. For those of mediocre ability part of the course was to be curtailed, and positions were to be found for them in lower schools. The poorest pupils were to be taught reading, writing, arithmetic and a little language and were to be prepared for positions of personal service. At the end of the four years this system broke down and no more "servitors" were received at the institution in Dessau. The attempt would only have tended to retain the poor type of valet as teachers in the elementary schools.[15]

Another form of training was that given to a few pupils by those of the clergy who had the ability and interest in education. This system received recognition and was recommended in the *Renewed School-ordinance* for the German town and rural schools of the Electorate of Saxony (section 13).[16] Dinter, who

[14]Kehr, Pädagogische Blätter, 1878, p. 331, ff.

[15]Schmid, Geschichte der Pädagogik, IV, 2, pp. 190, ff.

[16]Leuschke, Zur Geschichte der Lehrerbildungsfrage im Königreich Sachsen, p. 23.

later became the director of the normal school in Dresden-Friedrichstadt, gives an account in his autobiography of the work which he accomplished in the training of five pupils in this way.[17] But however well-meaning these efforts were, progress was checked through lack of means. Although the course of training as a general rule lasted two years the accommodation and the teaching staff were in most cases so limited that the two or three classes had to be taught together. Dinter, for example, had a three years' course at school in Dresden-Friedrichstadt, but was compelled to repeat his curriculum annually. When library facilities were very small, this practice had some advantages, but on the whole it must be admitted that it was uneconomical. The relations between the teachers and the students were very friendly. Dinter's reply to the critics, who found fault with his liberal attitude towards his pupils, was " Whoever expects too much seriousness from young fellows of seventeen to twenty, has at any rate no knowledge of men."

Although the salaries paid to teachers in those days were small and the position of a teacher still commanded very little respect, the students and teachers in the normal schools at that time had all the enthusiasm of pioneers. It was this spirit of earnestness and devotion which slowly and surely won the respect and support of the leading men of Germany. In 1794 all schools and universities were recognized as state institutions by the General Constitution of Prussia (*Allgemeine Landrecht*). And in the same year a Normal School Commission (*Seminarkommission*) was established in Saxony, and three years later an examination ordinance was promulgated for those who had completed a three years' course in a normal school. The institutions, however, still remained in private hands and were maintained mainly out of private funds, although the Prussian Government occasionally gave some contributions.

The first twenty years of the new century saw an increased activity in educational affairs in Germany. To the national and political causes was added the interest aroused by Pestalozzi's work. In 1803 J. E. Plamann[18] visited Burgdorf, where he remained several months. On his return to Berlin he established a

[17]Dinter, Autobiographie, pp. 169-190.
[18]Barnard, Pestalozzi and Pestalozzianism, p. 217.

school on the same system, which soon became the centre of German Pestalozzianism, and in 1805 he received royal recognition. In 1809 K. A. Zeller, a devoted student and follower of Pestalozzi, was summoned from Württemberg to Königsberg, where he conducted courses in pedagogy for clergy and teachers. He was instrumental in founding three normal schools in East Prussia. At the same time the government adopted the farsighted policy of sending young men to study the work of Pestalozzi at Yverdun for two or three years at the expense of the state.[19] Many of these later became directors of normal schools or school inspectors. Thus Henning became director at Cöslin, Preuss director at Karalene, Dreist became school inspector in Stettin and Kawerau in Cöslin. The Plamann institution in Berlin was also used to train teachers in Pestalozzian ideas. Here W. Harnisch spent some years at the expense of the state. He became first teacher in the normal school at Breslau, where he found two colleagues who had been students at Yverdun, and later he was appointed director of the normal school at Weissenfels. In Saxony Dinter strove to carry out the Pestalozzian ideals, and in Württemberg the new education was introduced by Denzel, who was director of the normal school at Esslingen. The twenty years after the disaster at Jena (1806) were marked by a rapid increase in the number of normal schools throughout Germany. In 1817 the Ministry for Public Worship, Education and Medical Affairs was separated from the Ministry of the Interior, with Von Altenstein at the head. In 1821 Dr. Ludolf Beckedorff was appointed to take charge of the section for normal schools, which now numbered twenty-eight. Acting on the principle that "to have good schools we must have good teachers," he devoted the six years during which he was in office to improving the status of teachers and to raising the standard of the candidates for the teaching profession. In 1820 the first *Regulations for Normal Schools* were published in Saxony, and recognised Latin and French as part of the curriculum of these institutions.

The two men who, more than others at this period, contributed to raise the professional status and to place the curriculum of the German normal schools on an intellectual basis were Harnisch and

---

[19]Monroe, W. S., The Pestalozzian Movement in the United States, ch. I. (Syracuse, 1907); Wilke, Diesterweg und die Lehrerbildung, p. 41; Berlin, 1890.

Diesterweg.[20] Different as the attitude of these men was, the one
being a strong pietist, while the other was just as strongly ration-
alistic, they joined in the view that the future teachers must have
an intellectual training not limited by the subjects which were
taught in the elementary schools. They also saw clearly that the
length of the normal school course must be extended to a uniform
period of three years. The teacher of the future must be taught
to think and not trained to be a machine. On these grounds they
both objected to the system of preparation for the normal schools
which then prevailed. This was obtained by a course at a special
preparatory school, which prepared candidates for the entrance
examinations at the normal schools, or by a system of pupil-
teacherships. The only suitable preparation which would have
satisfied them would have been a course in a higher elementary
school. The gymnasium was considered by both as totally un-
suitable to prepare for the normal schools. In this direction,
however, neither Harnisch nor Diesterweg was able to bring
about any reform. But in their main objects they met with the
greatest success. Apart from the progress which they made in
their own field, Harnisch at Weissenfels, and Diesterweg at Mörs
and later in Berlin, they contributed in no small measure to
arouse a strong professional feeling among the teachers throughout Germany. Associations began to be formed, demands for
higher education began to make themselves felt, and the greatest
interest was shown in further education. During the period
which preceded the Revolution of 1848 the teachers were agitat-
ing at meetings of their associations[21] and in the columns of the
educational magazines, a product of the quickened professional
feeling, and were definitely formulated at the National Assembly
held in Frankfort in 1848. Briefly these demands were: (a)
The abolition of clerical control. (b) The establishment of ministerial departments of education. (c) The abolition of preparatory institutions and the preparation of candidates for the normal
schools in higher elementary schools. (d) A higher intellectual
curriculum in the normal schools. (e) The removal of the
normal schools to university towns and the erection of the normal

[20]For Diesterweg consult Kreitz, Diesterweg und die Lehrerbildung.
Wittenberg, 1890; Wilke, Diesterweg und die Lehrerbildung, Berlin, 1890.
[21]Rissmann, Geschichte des deutschen Lehrervereins, p. 41. Berlin
1908.

schools into professional institutions. (f) The recognition of teachers as civil servants and exemption from the lower church duties. (g) Inspection of schools by professional men. (h) The inclusion of teachers on local school boards.

The Revolution failed but the teachers of Prussia thought that they might hope for reforms when in the following year the Ministry summoned a conference of twelve directors and teachers of normal schools to discuss the proposed reforms. But all hopes of obtaining their demands were shattered, when it was known that the King placed the responsibility of the recent disorders at the door of the normal schools and the teachers whom they had produced. The power of the reaction was now supreme throughout Germany, and it is a significant fact, illustrative as much of the strength of the reactionaries as of the premature character of the demands, that in Prussia only the proposals (f) and (h) have been realized up to the present.

The first consequence of the reaction was the retirement of Diesterweg, who had done so much to foster an independent spirit among the teachers. The further consequences soon appeared. In 1852 an administrative order was issued limiting the period of attendance at the normal schools to three years[22] and this was to be followed by apprenticeship to a country teacher, who would be responsible for the further education and the practical training of the candidates. In Prussia the expected *Regulations* were issued in 1854 (*Regulativa*, 1, *Okt.* 1854).[23] The responsibility for these regulations rests on Stiehl who directed the department for normal and elementary schools. Candidates for the normal schools were to receive their preparation privately from the pastors or teachers. The curriculum of the normal schools was limited to the subjects of the elementary schools. The aim of the normal schools was declared to be to give the pupils practical and theoretical instruction in religion, reading, the mother tongue, writing, arithmetic, singing, history, and nature study, without any attempt at scientific treatment. The reading of the German classics was forbidden. Training in the professional subjects was limited to *Schulkunde*. In this way political and clerical obscurantism and reaction triumphed over the results of enlightened progress.

---

[22]The course had been extended to four years in 1835.
[23]Schmid, Encykl., 10, 83-99.

The same principles of restriction and limitation characterize the *Regulations for the evangelical normal schools of the Kingdom of Saxony* of 1857.[24] In the same year Bavaria had issued regulations for normal schools based on those of Prussia. It is significant that it was during this period that the advisability of employing women teachers was discussed in Saxony[25] and that a state normal school for women teachers was established at Droyssig in Prussia in 1853, followed by a school in Saxony, which was opened at Callnberg in 1856.

The reactionaries had, however, made the mistake of going too far with their extreme measures. Their bitterest opponents, and among them Diesterweg, were ready to recognize such merits as could be discovered in the *Regulations* of 1854. The position of the normal schools was at least defined and uniformity was introduced. Stronger emphasis was laid on the importance of a thorough practical training in the practice schools, which were attached to the normal schools. Stress was laid on relating methods with the subject matter as taught in the class-rooms to the students. But nothing could compensate for the restrictions placed on the intellectual training. No question received so much attention in the professional magazines and at the meetings of the teachers' associations as that of the importance of a wider study of German literature. In 1859 Von Raumer retired from the position of Minister of Education. The immediate effect of this was that concessions began to be granted. In the same year there was an extension of mathematical curriculum in the normal schools. In 1861 permission was given by a ministerial decree to read the classical works of the national writers, although this had continued to be done privately in spite of the *Regulations*. About the same time the study of chemistry was introduced.[26] In Saxony there was also a change in the attitude of the government towards the normal schools. The *Ordinance for the admission of elementary school teachers to the university to obtain a higher professional training,* which was passed in 1865, was sufficient guarantee of a desire to raise the opportunities of the teachers

---

[24]Promulgated on June 15, 1859. This law excluded Latin, logic and psychology from the curriculum of the normal schools.

[25]Leuschke, Zur Geschichte der Lehrerbildungsfrage im Königreich Sachsen, p. 90.

[26]Kreitz, p. 119; Leuschke, ch. 9.

for further education. The ordinance only provided for the grant of the privilege to those who obtained an "Excellent" or "Good with distinction" in the examination for appointment as teacher and had already been actively engaged in school work. Admission was granted to a course at the University of Leipzig for two years, but at the end of the course candidates on passing an examination became eligible for appointment in a secondary school. A genuine wave of liberalism spread over Saxony. So far as possible attempts were made to meet the wishes of the teachers. Thus in 1866 the Minister of Culture summoned the directors of the normal schools to a conference on language instruction and throughout this period the Ministry of Culture was represented at the conferences and meetings of the teachers' associations, at which the improvement of the normal school course very often formed the subject of discussion.

In Prussia several circumstances combined to bring about, if not the revocation of the *Regulations* of 1854, at least a measure of reform. The sixties had seen the growth of commercial and industrial prosperity of the state and with it came a popular demand for better schools. The agitations of the teachers themselves could not be disregarded. Diesterweg had carried the campaign into the Lower House and had fought for the rights of the teachers almost up to his death in 1866. The war of 1870 and its successful issue also brought about the need of reorganization. In 1872 Falk, a man with a genuine interest in the education of the people and the welfare of the teachers, became Minister of Education. Two months after his appointment the *School Inspection Law* was passed, by which the schools were declared to be under the direct inspection of the state and the pastors could only exercise any control in so far as they received authorization from the government. The general educational reform was taken in hand almost immediately. In June a conference was held in Berlin to which the Minister had summoned representatives of political parties and the various types of schools. On October 15 the *General Regulations* were issued.[27] Here it is only necessary to enter into them so far as they concern the normal schools. The changes which directors had made on their own initiative since 1854 were recognized.

---

[27]Quoted in *extenso* in Schmid, Encykl., 10, 102-110.

The scope of the curriculum was extended in accordance with the demands of the teachers. The importance of the study of German literature was recognized and with it the need of good school libraries. The scientific studies were extended and now included nature study, physics and chemistry. Religious instruction was curtailed and, though still forming an important part of the curriculum, did not equal the amount prescribed by the last *Regulations*. But the principle was still retained that every lesson must be given in such a form that it could be reproduced in the elementary school. In other words every lesson must be a lesson in method. Nor was any encouragement given to study a foreign language, the mark of higher education in those days. Latin and foreign languages were made optional, with the reservation that only the more gifted students should take them up and begin with French. To meet the higher requirements and standards of the normal schools the state recognized preparatory instituions with courses lasting from two to three years, provided that they agreed to submit to inspection.

The *Regulations* met with the general approval of the teachers, and with the institution of promotion examinations the greatest enthusiasm and activity in further training manifested themselves. New questions and new demands arose, but all were in the direction of an extension of opportunities for advanced study. These the Prussian government has not yet granted and in this has remained somewhat behind many of the smaller states. The *Regulations* of 1872 remained in force until they were superseded by the *Regulations and Course of Study* of 1901. In spite, however, of regulations and prescriptions with liberal tendencies, the spirit and the traditions which had been established during the century could not be eradicated and the influence of clericalism is still to be noticed in the normal schools. The direction of the normal schools and the inspection of elementary education are still preponderatingly in the hands of theologians. The attitude of the educational authorities in Prussia may be understood from the persistent refusal to follow the lead established by Saxony and to recognize the normal schools as a part of the system of higher education. The only concession in this direction has been the recognition of the final leaving examination of a normal school as a qualification for the one year volunteer military service. In other words the graduates of normal schools obtain at the age of twenty a privilege which is granted at the end of six years' study to those who attend a secondary school.

In Saxony the new era for normal schools was ushered in by the *Ordinance for Normal Schools for Elementary School Teachers* of July 14th, 1873.[28] So far as the curriculum is concerned this measure fully put into operation the wishes expressed by the Pedagogical Society of Chemnitz in 1866.[29] With a few minor changes this Ordinance was embodied in the *Law on Gymnasiums, Real Schools and Normal Schools* of August 22nd, 1876, which with the detailed directions for the operation of the law, issued on January 29th, 1877, included the normal schools among the institutions for higher education. Since this law is still in operation, it will be treated in the following pages in some detail. But it is important at this point to emphasize the contrast between the manifestation of a liberal attitude in Prussia and in Saxony.

The normal school system of Bavaria as at present organized is based on the *Regulation for the Training of Teachers in the Kingdom of Bavaria*. This system is representative of a type which differs from the systems of Prussia and Saxony and will be dealt with in subsequent chapters.

The history of the training of women teachers is limited to the last century.[30] Not that women had not previously played an important part in the work of the school. Female teaching orders had existed in the thirteenth century and these gave instruction to poor and rich. Further, among the *Winkelschulen* there were also dame schools.[31] Nor did the guilds set their faces against the keeping of school by the widows of former members, though it was usual in such cases to employ an assistant who had served his apprenticeship. In Lübeck there was a guild of women teachers of reading.[32] In a Regulation issued in Prussia in 1738 women were allowed to keep school, provided they obtained the necessary license from the town authorities, in which they might teach boys up to seven years of age and girls as long as their parents were willing to keep them at school.

---

[28]Kretzschmar, J. F., Höheres Schulwesen in Sachsen.

[29]Leuschke, pp. 111–115.

[30]Herber, Das Lehrerinnenwesen in Deutschland, pp. 7-12; Lexis, Das Unterrichtswesen im deutschen Reich, vol. II, 282-8.

[31]Fischer, p. 206. [32]Fischer, p. 252.

The earliest training course for women teachers was established in the diocese of Münster in 1783 and was under the direction of Bernhard Overberg. In 1832 the first normal schools for the training of women were established in Münster and Berlin, and both were attached to the girls' high schools. The number increased rapidly within the next four years.[33] In 1845 the first examination ordinance for women teachers was issued in Prussia.[34] In 1852 the first Prussian normal school for women under state supervision was opened at Droyssig and in Saxony in 1856 at Callnberg. In the fifties the number of women teachers rose owing to a dearth of male teachers. Institutions which prepared for the examination rapidly increased. No regulations were passed for the guidance of the Prussian normal schools for women with the exception of that at Droyssig. In 1874 new regulations for the examination of women were issued and have remained in force up to the present with some slight modifications. No sharp distinction was drawn between the preparation given in the female normal schools for service in elementary or high schools for girls. The examinations and the organization of the normal schools for women will be dealt with more fully later. Here it need only be mentioned that the tendency at present is to separate the training of candidates for elementary and high schools. In Saxony, however, a distinction is made in the examinations for the two positions but the preparation for both is given in the same institutions, which were organized in 1876. In Bavaria no distinction has been made between the training of men and women since 1868 with the exception of some differences in the details of the curriculum.

Thus the evolution of the German elementary school teachers into a professional class is a phase of the history of the development of the political emancipation of the German people. Both movements represent a struggle against obscurantism and clerical domination. The teachers are still far from the attainment of the position which their predecessors claimed almost a century ago. Any attempt to move forward in the process of natural evolution is blocked by reactionary opponents, and this accounts for the fact that the normal schools of Germany suffer more from the influence of tradition than most German institutions.

---

[33]Barnard, German Normal Schools, p. 108, ff.

[34]Herber, pp. 26-28.

CHAPTER II

ADMINISTRATIVE AUTHORITIES

In the following chapter it is proposed to deal only with the German administrative authorities in so far as they come into relation with the teachers of the elementary schools, with the normal schools and the whole question of the training of the elementary school teachers and their appointment and conditions of service.

Within the limits mentioned the Imperial government is only concerned with the maintenance of the standards of the examinations on which the privilege of one-year military service as a volunteer (*Einjährig Freiwilliger*) is granted. Otherwise the organization of education is left to the states individually.

With the exception of the fact that the King has the power of appointing the directors of the normal schools the chief authority in educational affairs in Prussia is vested in the Ministry for Public Worship, Education and Medical Affairs. At the head of this department stands the Minister who is a member of the cabinet. He is appointed by and responsible to the crown. In the Lower House he represents his department, which has competence in three fields as is denoted in its title. In educational matters the Minister is responsible for the drawing up of the budget and for the expenditures. In questions of conflicting authority and in the decision of all appeals on educational matters he acts as the final court of appeal. Since there is no codified legislation on education in Prussia his power of issuing administrative orders, of drawing up courses of study and of issuing regulations renders his position one of considerable importance and responsibility, and a reactionary Minister of Education may cause considerable trouble and dissatisfaction, as happened in the case of the recent Minister Studt, famous for his orders to put on the brake (Bremserlass). The orders, regulations, rescripts and decisions (*Erlass, Regulativ, Verfügung, Bestimmung*) issued by the Minister have the force of law. These are published in the *Centralblatt für die gesamte Unterrichtsverwaltung,* which all school authorities are obliged to take.[1] The power of making certain appointments and ratifying others as well as of conferring titles on teachers is vested in the Minister. Immediately under the Minister is an Under-secretary of State.

For purposes of administration the educational section of the ministry is divided into two departments, each under a director. One department deals with university, higher, technical and art education. The other controls elementary and normal schools, the education of girls, physical training, and institutions for idiots, blind, deaf and dumb. The authority of these departments is largely delegated to administrative bodies with power over areas of varying extent from the provinces to the local districts.[2]

Prussia is divided into thirteen provinces. For educational matters the chief authority in each province is the Chief President of the province assisted by a board consisting of four or five school councillors, inspectors and administrative officials. The Chief President is responsible for the smooth working of the administrative machinery of his province. With the aid of the Provincial School Board (*Provinzialschulkollegium*) he appoints the commissions to hold examinations for middle-school teachers and school principals. Subject to the ratification of the Minister he appoints teachers to the normal schools, with the exception of the director, and to preparatory institutions maintained by the state. He decides on all financial matters affecting teachers; he may compel teachers in elementary and middle schools to retire on a pension and he has the authority to grant extended leave of absence. Under his direction the board has charge of all branches of higher school education. It directs the appointment, promotion, discipline, suspension or dismissal of teachers in higher schools, including normal schools and preparatory institutions. It examines text-books and with the consent of the Minister may issue new books, when necessary. All statutes and regulations for the internal management of schools

---

[1]*Central-Blatt für die gesamte Unterrichtsverwaltung,,* 1883, p. 503.

[2]Kretzschmar, Handbuch des Preussischen Schulrechts, pp. 6, 7; Bremen, Die Preussische Volksschule, pp. 163-4; Russell, German Higher Schools, ch. V.

must have the approval of the board. Further, the board regulates and supervises the leaving examinations from high schools (*Abiturientenexamen*) and from normal schools as well as the examination for the permanent appointment of elementary school teachers. Twice a year reports of the work of the board must be sent in to the Minister.[3]

A further subdivision of Prussia is into royal counties (*Königliche Regierungen*)[4] of which there are thirty-six in number. In each county there is a department for churches and schools, (*Abteilung für Kirchen und Schulen*). Generally speaking the control of the county authority is confined to elementary, middle and private schools and philanthropic institutions. The department for churches and schools appoints teachers to the elementary schools on royal domains and ratifies the appointments made by other patrons and school committees. It audits church and school accounts and supervises the operation of all school laws and ministerial rescripts. At the request of local bodies the department may inquire into local conditions and establish school districts. Further, it may supervise the conduct, public and private, of teachers and grants short terms of leave. The county boards are presided over by the County President, and include chief county councillors, county councillors and professional members. Every councillor must make an annual tour of his county and report his observation, which are included in the report of the department. The Chief President of the province acts as the intermediary between the provincial and county boards by a ministerial decree holds a combined meeting of the provincial and county boards once in two years.[5]

The local authorities[6] with power over more restricted areas and standing in closer relation to those who use the schools are in towns the School Deputation (*Stadtsschuldeputation*) and in rural districts the School Committee (*Schulvorstand*). The school deputation is representative of most of the interests of a town, the only restriction being that supporters of the social democratic party are not eligible. The deputation consists of

---

[3]Kretzschmar, pp. 18, 19; Bremen, pp. 164, 165 and 170-2.
[4]Kretzschmar, pp. 12-17; Bremen, p. 165 and pp. 176-185.
[5]1888. See Bremen, p. 164.
[6]Bremen, pp. 517-528; Plüschke, P., Die städtischen Schuldeputationen und ihr Geschäftskreis, pp. 10-69.

from one to three executive officials of the town, nominated by the
mayor; an equal number of town councillors; professional members interested in education, selected by the first two classes already mentioned; representatives of denominations and royal
schools, which may be located in the town. By ministerial decrees of 1897 and 1902, which have since received the authority
of law (1906), among the professional representatives there must
be included a teacher or principal of a school, and if the number
of professional members exceeds four there may be two teachers
on the board, although in such a case one of the teachers may be
female and from an elementary school under the control of the
deputation.[7]   The members must receive the approval of the
county authorities and hold office for six years. In addition to
the above the district school inspector (*Kreisschulinspektor*) of
the district and the director of education, who in the larger
towns often performs the duties of the district inspector, also
have seats on the deputation as government representatives.[8]

The competence of the school deputation[9] extends over the
internal and external arrangement of the schools, more particularly elementary and middle schools, their equipment, the compulsory attendance of children of school age, and the provision
of sufficient and satisfactory school buildings. With the approval
of the county authority it appoints teachers and school principals
and arranges salary scales. It draws up the annual financial
budget and approves courses of study and text-books. The approval of a higher authority is, however, required for the acts of
the school deputation. In no case has the deputation any disciplinary authority over teachers nor can it interfere in the actual
conduct of a school. The professional members may visit the
schools, take note of the progress of the pupils, and make suggestions to the principal, but nothing more. In visiting girls' high
schools, which are under the charge of the town they are em-
powered to coopt women who take an interest in educational
matters. An annual report of the work of the deputation must
be sent in to the county department for schools.

The school deputation may delegate its authority to commissions. Of these the most important are the School Commissions

[7]Plüschke, p. 62.
[8]Ibid., p. 63.
[9]Ibid., pp. 107, 108 and 113-116.

(*Schulkommission*) which act virtually as managers of single schools. They consist of a town official nominated by the mayor or another member as chairman, a local school inspector,[10] if there is one, a pastor of the denomination represented by a majority of the pupils in the school, a member of the staff of the school selected by the deputation, and representatives of the inhabitants of the locality in which the school is situated. The commissions look after the interest of the school to which they are assigned and see that its equipment is not behind that of other schools of the town, and have a voice in the selection of a teacher for their school. Among other duties they arrange parents' evenings and look after the poorer pupils of the school.[11]

The School Committee[12] in rural communities consists of the mayor, where there is such an official, or a corresponding official, a teacher selected by the supervising authority, the pastor of the denomination to which a majority of the pupils belong, and from one to six representatives of the local inhabitants. The committee serves to keep awake local interest in the school. It fixes the budget for the maintenance of the school and provides the ways and means for this purpose. It is responsible for the satisfactory equipment of the school and the salaries of the teachers. The provision of a school-building, its ventilation and heating, the regular attendance of the pupils, the promotion of parents' evenings, lectures and school festivals are within the competence of the committee. Further, the committee serves to bring particular local needs to the notice of the district school inspector or to the higher authority, the county department for education. Such local needs include a rearrangement of the time-table or the vacations, or the discharge of pupils from school before they have reached the statutory age.

The inspection of schools is entrusted to district school inspectors and local school inspectors. The former (*Kreisschulinspektoren*) are appointed by the minister on the recommendation of the county authorities.[13] Nominally they should be appointed from among normal school teachers with academic or normal school training, or from among principals of elementary schools.

[10]Ibid., pp, 665, 666 and 707.
[11]Ibid., pp. 706, 707.
[12]Ibid., pp. 707-710.
[13]Bremen, p. 189.

In practice, however, the office is usually given to normal school teachers who have had a university training, or to clergymen. One of the chief demands of the teachers, reiterated again and again since 1848, is for the establishment of a professional inspectorate selected from those who have a knowledge of the actual conditions and requirements of elementary education from practical experience.[14] As at present constituted the inspection of schools is largely in the hands of men whose main duties lie in other walks of life. The number of inspectors who devote themselves entirely to the duties of inspection is gradually increasing, although as will be seen from the following table[15] the increase is very slow:

YEAR	INSPECTORS OF SCHOOLS EXCLUSIVELY		INSPECTING SCHOOLS AS AN ADDITIONAL DUTY		TOTAL
	Number	Per cent.	Number	Per cent.	
1882.........	181	20.11	719	79.89	900
1897.........	229	21.01	861	78.99	1090
1892.........	246	20.26	968	79.74	1214
1897.........	277	22.30	965	77.70	1242
1902.........	316	25.77	914	74.23	1230
1907.........	331	26.00	941	74.00	1272

The local school inspectors (*Ortsschulinspektoren*) are in most cases the local pastors except in large graded schools where the function of the local inspector is exercised by the principal of the school. The strongest objections are expressed against this form of inspection, which is claimed by the church as a traditional right. The opposition of the teachers is based on the ground that this practice subordinates them to an authority which lacks the necessary knowledge and training to enter with sympathy into the work of the school. The opposition in no way involves any antagonism to religious training in the school, but it is felt that the influence of the pastor ought not to extend beyond that.

---

[14]Rissmann, pp. 35, 88, 92, 93, 95, 101, 169, 206, 216, 225, where reports of the resolutions passed on the subject of professional inspection since 1848 are given.

[15]*Rept.*, *U. S. Com. Educ.*, 1908, p. 188.

Recognizing that such objections were reasonable the government by a decree issued in 1842 instituted a short training course for candidates for the ministry.[16] In 1889 an ordinance was published by the Minister containing new regulations on this course. Every theological candidate between his first and second examination must present himself at a normal school for a training of six weeks in order to acquaint himself with the nature of the instruction given in a Prussian elementary school. Those who have already had some experience in teaching in any type of school are exempted, as well as those who have had a course in educational principles at a theological seminary. Not more than twelve candidates may attend the same course. During their attendance in the normal school they are under the direction of the director of the school. The aim of the course is to prepare the future pastor for the duties of school supervision. Special attention must be paid to the practice-school, and to the work in the normal schools in order to obtain some idea of the nature and scope of the training of a teacher and the significance of the different branches of the curriculum, as well as some knowledge of the theory and principles of education. It is expected of the candidates that they should make themselves acquainted with the regulations dealing with the elementary schools. The director of the normal school draws up a program for the course with special care that there should be some continuity in the work pursued by the candidates. He holds conferences with the candidates and directs them to the best educational writings. At least once during the course the candidates must give a lesson in the practice-school in the presence of the director and the faculty of the normal school. Wherever there is an opportunity the candidate must make some study of institutions for the blind, the deaf and the dumb. At the end of the course the director reports to the Provincial School Board, which in turn forwards the report to the Provincial Consistory. If a report is unsatisfactory, the latter may compel a candidate to repeat a course. This practice may be well-meant but it is hardly a satisfactory preparation to qualify interference with a teacher who has had a similar training for three years and has the professional attitude. Moreover the course is not taken seriously. Very little attention

---

[16]*Central-Blatt*, 1889, p. 537.

is usually paid by the candidates to the work of the class-room and the lack of sympathy is often to be noticed in the laughter which is indulged in by the academically trained candidates at the expense of the normal school pupils. On the whole the demand of the Prussian teacher for professional inspection is fully justified.

The duties of the district school inspector are not officially prescribed by the central authority but may be gathered from the instructions issued by the county department of Cöslin.[17]   The inspector acts in an advisory capacity to the local school inspector and the local authorities but has no power to restrict their influence.   He exercises disciplinary authority over the teachers, whom he may warn, fine or censure, and has power to grant leave of absence for a limited period.   He must visit the schools at least once a year, examine in about three branches of the curriculum, and inspect the records of the work done by the teacher. All matters referring to the school building are within his province.   He holds conferences of the teachers of the district and superintends the preparatory training of teachers.   Reports must be made to the county authority.   The duties of the local school inspectors are much the same as those of the district inspectors, with this difference that the local inspectors are in more intimate touch with the schools.   In addition to superintending the general conduct of the teachers in and out of the school and reporting any dereliction of duty, the local inspectors also hold the examinations of the pupils of the schools under their charge.   All reports of the local inspectors go to the district inspectors.

The educational systems from the point of view of administration are so much alike in the three most important states of Germany that it will here only be necessary to point out such differences as do exist.   A striking feature of the Saxon system is the predominance of professional influence.   The recognition of normal school training and a period of service in an elementary school as a qualification for admission to the University of Leipzig has not only fostered professional interest and provided a strong stimulus for advanced study but has put a large number of men with experience of elementary school conditions and aca-

---

[17]Regierungs-Bezirk Cöslin, *Amtliches Schulblatt*, 1897, Nr. 6; quoted in Kretzschmar, F., p. 58.

demic training at the disposal of the government for higher administrative positions. A strong factor in the Saxon system is the annual meeting[18] of school inspectors to which well-qualified schoolmen are invited as well as representatives of the clerical and medical professions. At this conference the annual reports of the inspectors are made the subject of discussion. For administrative purposes Saxony is much more compact, and since the interests are predominatingly commercial and industrial, presents far more uniform conditions than either Prussia or Bavaria. Owing to her size Saxony can dispense with one of the intermediate educational authorities found in the other two countries. Hence the county subdivision is not found and the duties of the Provincial School Boards of Prussia and of the corresponding board of Bavaria (*Kreisregierung*) are performed by the District Inspection Board (*Bezirksinspektion*). In the towns these boards consist of the town council and the district inspector, and elsewhere of this official and the executive commissioner (*Amtshauptmann*). Although the pastors are *ex officio* members of the local boards (*Schulvorstand*), their influence is largely limited to the supervision of religious instruction.[19]

The Bavarian system is marked by clerical influence which is even more extensive than in Prussia.[20] On the local school boards (*Ortsschulbehörde*) the pastor is chairman and in performing the functions of local school inspector may exercise his authority over any part of the instruction. Similarly the district school inspector (*Distriktschulinspektor*) is always a clergyman with some knowledge of pedagogy, and his appointment by the district school board (*Distriktschulbehörde*) must have the approval of the church authorities.[21] The towns,[22] however, are only subject to the authority of the *Kreisregierung*, which corresponds to the Provincial School Board. As in Prussia the towns are divided into wards with separate boards (*Stadtbezirksschulinspektion*), all of which with the addition of the mayor and the director of schools, if one is employed, constitute the town school board (*Stadtsschulkommission*). It will be noticed that the constitution of this board differs from that of the town

---

[18]Seydewitz, Das königliche Sächsische Volksschulgesetz, pp. 123-130.
[19]Seydewitz, p. 95.
[20]Stingl and Englmann, Handbuch des Bayerischen Volksschulrechts, pp. 15-34. [21]Ibid., pp. 45-93. [22]Ibid., pp. 97-105.

boards in Prussia. The larger administrative areas[23] (*Kreis*) are formed out of several districts and the administration of school matters is in the hands of an executive official (*Kreis-schulreferent*) who is assisted by a professional inspector and a board consisting of representatives of middle and girls' schools, normal schools, the clergy, laymen and elementary schools (*Kreisschulkommission*). There are eight of these commissions throughout the country. The supreme authority is vested in a ministry which has charge of ecclesiastical as well as educational affairs (*Ministerium für Kirchen—und Schulangelegenheiten*). Since 1905 a national commission including representatives of the district inspectors, normal, girls', trade and elementary schools, the clergy and lay members of school boards has been established.[24]

The administrative principle observed in the three states is decentralization with a system of checks. In the control of elementary education there are concerned bodies with power over the single school district responsible to authorities with power over still larger areas until the supreme central organization is reached in the ministry. While the local committee builds, equips and maintains the schools and pays the teachers in part, another body sanctions the appointment of teachers and inspects the schools, still another is responsible for the training and examination of teachers, while the central authority acts as a final court of appeal in cases of dispute and administrative difficulty, fixes the curriculum, establishes standards of attainment and so far as possible equalizes the burden of school support. But although the administrative machinery for securing local initiative is perfect, it is to be noticed that this is confined to the externals of school management. Anything like an attempt to arrange the curriculum of an elementary school in response to local needs and conditions is unknown. Hence one school is much like another within any one state. Whether a growing professional sense and the presence of teachers on local boards, now demanded by law in all states, will ultimately succeed in breaking down the principle of bureaucratic control of the curriculum remains an open question.

---

[23]Ibid., pp. 112-127.

[24]*Pädagogisches Jahrbuch*, 1905, p. 111." This may be compared with the consultative committees in England and France.

CHAPTER III

THE PREPARATORY TRAINING OF TEACHERS

An important factor in a good system of training teachers is to secure that the candidates on entering the normal school have had an adequate preparation. The practice almost universal in Germany is to begin the training of teachers or rather to make the selection of candidates for the teaching profession about their fourteenth year. Technically speaking, however, only Prussia and Bavaria have a distinct system of preparatory institutions (*Präparandenanstalten*). But since these, though in administration distinct from the normal schools, exist only to act as feeders for them, there is no reason for giving a separate treatment to the first three classes of the six-year normal school in Saxony, which begins with the fourteenth year. It is claimed[1] for the Prussian and Bavarian systems of keeping the preparatory schools distinct from the normal schools that they possess the advantages of small institutions. The number of pupils to be dealt with is small and uniform aims can better be carried out. The directors and instructors can devote the whole of their attention to a smaller group. The separation of the boys from the young men is better for character-training, since the appropriate methods can be applied to each. The same arguments could of course be employed for splitting any school course of six or more years' duration into two parts. The tendency in both Prussia and Bavaria is to unite the preparatory school more intimately with the normal school in the same way as is done in Saxony. There is no doubt that the larger institution makes for administrative efficiency. There is an absence of that break in the middle of the six years with the heavy strain of an examination. Nor is any time lost through transference to a new situation. Further, a union into a six years' course admits of the employ-

---

[1]Rein, Zur Reform der Lehrerbildung, *Jahrbuch des Vereins für wissenschaftlische Pädagogik* (Dresden 1902).

ment of specialist teachers, which is highly desirable where advanced instruction is given and which cannot be introduced where there are only three classes. There is no doubt that of the three systems that in Saxony is best from the point of view of organization.

The preparatory institutions of Prussia, although all working under the uniform curriculum issued in 1901, fall into three types, according to their administration—state, municipal, and private. At present there is a tendency for the state to increase the preparatory institutions under its control. In the state and municipal institutions the staff consists of a principal and two teachers. The principal must have the same qualifications as a normal school teacher, that is, he must have passed the examinations for teachers in middle schools and for principals in elementary schools.[2] The assistant teachers[3] must have passed the examination for permanent appointment in an elementary school. An attempt is being made to raise the qualifications for the latter, but is not likely to succeed until the salaries are increased. These positions are usually taken by teachers who desire ultimately to enter the service of the normal schools. The salary of the principals of preparatory institutions ranges from 2100-3800 M. ($525-950), that of the assistants from 1500-2400 M. ($375-600).[4] These teachers are state servants and as such are entitled to all the privileges of state servants, such as a pension and provision for their widows and orphans.

The private preparatory institutions are in most cases attached to normal schools. Originally these were established by the faculty of the normal schools as commercial ventures as well as with the desire to secure properly prepared candidates for the normal school. Since 1892, however, the establishment of institutions of this type must have the approval of the Minister.[5] The administration in this case is in the hands of the director of the normal school, with which the institution is connected. In addition there are usually two assistant teachers, whose appointment must be sanctioned by the Provincial School Board, but the director and instructors in the normal school are permitted

---

[2]Bremen, p. 267.
[3]Lexis, III, p. 253.
[4]Bremen, p. 270.
[5]Ibid., pp. 245-247.

within certain restrictions to give instruction. The salaries are somewhat on the same scale as in the state and municipal institutions, but for the time being the teachers are not state servants, although their years of service in a private preparatory institution are counted, if they return to a regular school. By the same decree of 1892 the remuneration which the director and normal school instructors may receive for their services in the preparatory institution is fixed, and any money that is left over after the expenses of management have been paid must be applied to the support of poor pupils. A biennial report of the work of these institutions must be sent in to the Minister.[6]

School fees are charged in all the preparatory institutions, varying from 36 M. a year in the state and municipal institutions to 100 M. in the private. Where the pupils board in the institution—only a very small number, however—from 400 to 600 M. a year are charged. Poor pupils receive support, but this in no case amounts to more than 25 M. a month.

All candidates for entry into the preparatory institutions must send an application[7] to the director or principal, accompanied by certificates of baptism, health and vaccination endorsed by a state-recognized doctor, and reports on general school work and conduct. Candidates must be not less than fourteen years of age. There is an entrance examination, both written and oral, in the subjects of the elementary school.[8] Particular emphasis is laid on the oral test. The examination usually takes place at the beginning of the normal school year, Easter in most parts of Prussia. Where the examination is held at a different period it is complained that inferior candidates who failed to pass into other institutions present themselves.[9] The normal number of pupils in a preparatory institution is fixed at thirty for each class in the three years' course.

Whatever the administrative character of a preparatory institution may be, they all conform in the matter of inner organization and curriculum to the *Regulations and Course of Study* of 1901,[10] which introduced uniformity into the training given in

---

[6]Ibid., p. 247.
[7]Ibid., p. 241.
[8]Ibid., p. 241.
[9]E.g. in the Rhineland and Westphalia.
  Rept. U. S. Com. Educ., 1903, pp. 1233-1237.

the preparatory institutions. The question is approached from two points of view, the origin of the pupils and the aim of the course. Since the pupils are drawn not only from different types of elementary schools, varying from the ungraded village school to the fully graded town school, but also in a few cases from middle or even high schools, the first year must be spent in bringing all the pupils to the same standard of attainment on the basis of the work of an upper grade in an elementary school. At the other end the preparatory institutions since 1901 form an organic whole with the normal schools, and so far as possible a great part of the academic training is given there. Some part of the curriculum previously taught in the first two years of the normal school course were transferred to the preparatory institutions and there brought to a conclusion. Among these subjects are biblical history, catechism and hymns, elementary grammar and arithmetic, ancient history, natural history, and writing. While the *Regulations* aimed to secure so far as possible a separation of academic from professional instruction, it may be questioned whether they have not succeeded in overburdening pupils in training at an earlier age in their career.

The subjects of the curriculum in the preparatory institutions are religion, German and a foreign language, history, mathematics, natural science and geography, writing, drawing, music and gymnastics.[11]

As may be expected from the historical development of the training of teachers in Germany and their present position as assistants to the pastors, considerable emphasis is laid on religious instruction. While it is not necessary to go into any details on the scope of this subject, it may be said that a disproportionate amount of the time is devoted to it. The results are astounding for the amount which is memorized. Passages can be quoted by the pupils by chapter and verse, but as a general rule more time is devoted to the memorizing of the subject matter than to the character-forming elements in it.

Under German are included reading, grammar, and written and oral expression. Great stress is laid on the eradication of dialectical peculiarities and the use of pure German. While the reading is fairly extensive, it is almost entirely confined to the use of a " reader " containing selections of a very miscellaneous

----

[11] For details of the curriculum see the *Rept. U. S. Com. Educ.*, 1903.

character in prose and poetry. Attention is paid to both form and content, but in the treatment of poems the tendency to analyze and to dwell on the parts to the detriment of the whole is marked. Literary history as such is not taught apart from the selections from the classical productions contained in the reader. Only one drama is definitely assigned in the course of study, but the pupils are encouraged to supplement their school by outside reading. In the absence of good library facilities and through lack of time this provision can hardly be put into practice. Written and oral composition are based on the work done in the classroom. A characteristic of the German class-room is the attention devoted to oral expression on the part of the pupils. On the other hand, although the pupils are given frequent opportunities for speaking, they rarely get beyond a repetition of what the teacher has said, and in many cases exact verbal repetition is insisted upon. The occasions for spontaneous expression from the pupils are as rare as the asking of a question. Although the use of text-books has been eliminated, their place has been taken by the dictations of the teacher. It is true that the pupils are not allowed to take notes, but their attention while the teacher is talking is so acute that the reproductions are very faithful. In spite of the care devoted to the teaching of grammar, great difficulty is found in eradicating mistakes from the written composition, which in most cases are due to peculiarities of dialect. The teaching of grammar is of the type familiar to those who have studied Latin, and as much care is bestowed by the German pupils to the exceptions as by any foreign student of the language.

French is the foreign language most frequently taught, though English is recognized as an alternative. Little need be said about the teaching of French, except that as at present taught both in the preparatory institutions and in the normal schools it is merely a waste of time to retain it on the program. Whether it is that the pupils are too old, when they begin the study of a foreign language, or that the teachers themselves are inadequately prepared, success is rarely attained. Generally the pronunciation is very poor and the knowledge of the grammar unsatisfactory. This state of things is unfortunate, as it is seized upon by those who are opposed to a more liberal training of the teachers as an instance of the poor capacities of a class. But it would be unjust to compare pupils in these institutions with those in the regular high schools, where languages are begun at an earlier age and are taught by specialists. It must be added, however, that little importance is attached to the foreign language in the examinations, either for entrance into the normal school or in the leaving examination, which serves as the first teachers' examination.

Just as religious instruction is calculated to instil a reverence for the divine, so the aim of the teaching of history is to train the sense of national duty and loyalty to the reigning house. In addition to German history some attention is given to the chief events in Greek and Roman history. The method employed is mainly of the drum and trumpet variety with a strong emphasis on the dates. Insisting on this point, one teacher thus admonished his class, "Be careful of your dates, or your history will not be on a secure basis." There is no attempt to trace larger movements or to enunciate broad principles. Like the other subjects history is largely a matter for memorizing.

No subject is taught so well as mathematics, and here the influence of Pestalozzianism can still be traced. In arithmetic the aim is to ensure accuracy and certainty in dealing with numbers. The examples are based on the needs of practical life with which the future teacher will have to deal. Considerable emphasis is laid on mental arithmetic. In the third year the pupils are introduced to algebra or "arithmetic with letters," and the connection between the two is clearly brought out. Geometry is also taught with considerable ability and affords one of the few occasions on which the pupils are permitted to do a little independent thinking.

Natural science, which includes elementary botany, zoology, and physics as well as geography, belongs to the information subjects. Long lists of details and names are given, or simple experiments are performed by the teacher and the pupils must learn by heart or must be able, when called upon, to give an account of the experiment. Laboratory work is unknown in physics. In nature study the pupils are encouraged to collect plants on their excursions and these are named and classified at the next lesson. In geography the pupils display a skillful use of maps, but in general the topographical and political sides of the subject play an altogether too important part.

An unnecessary amount of time is devoted to writing as a separate subject of study, and is continued for the three years.

Although the official course of study prescribes practice in writing on the blackboard, this desirable training is too often neglected through lack of blackboard space.

Perhaps no subject usurps so much time as music. The importance attached to this subject is as in the case of religion largely traditional and is a survival of the time when the teachers acted as precentors and organists. The subject now embraces vocal music, violin, pianoforte, organ and harmony. There is an exemption for students who do not possess pronounced ability from playing the organ, but very few pupils avail themselves of this. Although the subject is taught exceedingly well, most frequently by specialists, there seems to be a sacrifice of practical common sense to principle in compelling all pupils to learn every branch. Nor do the results justify the expenditure of time. The violin playing, which is intended to enable teachers to accompany their classes in singing, rarely attains a quality which would justify its retention in the class-room. Nor is the amount of time spent on drill and talking about the technique and theory likely to train the aesthetic side. The subject has been frequently attacked recently and there will probably be some change in the matter of requirements.

Drawing like music is taught by specialists in most cases. It is interesting in this connection to notice that the work of writers on the method of the subject in this country have attracted considerable attention. Usually the teacher is hampered by the lack of a satisfactory supply of models. Some part of the work is correlated with the other subjects, but the teachers of drawing jealously guard their subject from being made the servant of all the rest. More will be said on this subject later in dealing with it in the normal schools.

A necessary antidote against the high temperature and the foul air usually found in the class-rooms, where windows are kept closed even in summer, are the gymnastic exercises. Here, however, it has been noticed that the pupils of one preparatory institution were drilled in an overheated and dusty gymnasium with all the windows shut at the very centre for the training of specialist teachers of gymnastics. It must be added that swimming and skating are permitted as alternatives to a part of the gymnastic exercises.

Throughout there is apparent a spirit of dogmatism on the part of the teachers and an exercise of authority which cannot fail to be cramping and narrowing to the intellect of their pupils. No one reading the course of study and the methodical instructions could find any objections whatever to them. Unfortunately the spirit of the instructions is too often sacrificed in order to cover the amount of the work which is prescribed. The pupils in the preparatory institutions are overburdened with work largely because so much importance is attached to memorizing everything that is assigned. How much time is left for recreation may be seen from the time-tables, of which a copy is given.[12] Where the pupils board at the school, they have at any rate the advantage of retiring to bed at a definite hour. The externs, however, are not so carefully supervised in their own homes. If the proposal to unite the preparatory institutions more intimately with the normal schools were put into operation, there would be a relaxation of the present strain, for apart from the extent of the curriculum the evil of preparing for the entrance examination into the normal schools and the responsibility of the teachers make themselves felt.

Although Saxony[13] maintains a normal school course beginning at 14 and continuing for six years without the distinction into preparatory institutions and normal school proper, there is no reason why the first three years of the course should not be treated in this chapter. The entrance qualifications are the same as in Prussia, that is, candidates must be not less than 14 years of age and must be able to pass an examination in the subjects of a graded school (*mittlere Volksschule*). In addition to the certificates demanded in Prussia all candidates must sign a declaration (*Revers*) of their willingness to accept any appointment offered to them by the school authorities for three years after leaving the normal school on pain of paying 120 M. for each year spent in the school. A similar declaration is signed by the Prussian candidates on their entrance into the normal school proper. No fees are charged in Saxony, but the expenses of board and lodging, which amount on an average to 205 M. a year, are borne by the

---

[12]See appendix.

[13]Kretzschmar, J. F. Höheres Schulwesen, in Sachsen, p. 86 and pp. 379-384.

pupils unless they receive some government support. There are usually twenty to twenty-five pupils in a whole school in receipt of support, but in no case is the full amount of the cost of board and lodging paid.

The Saxon normal schools are regulated by a law[14] of Aug. 22, 1876, and the instructions for the operation of the law issued on Jan. 29, 1877.[15] The curriculum is the same as that of the Prussian preparatory institutions and normal schools with the exception that Latin takes the place of French. But the similarity between the two states ends here, for there is an entirely different spirit in the class-rooms of the Saxon normal schools. In the first place the teachers up to about fifty per cent. have had academic training in addition to their experience as elementary school teachers. Hence many of these are specialists in one or more fields. A second feature is the absence of the tone of the drill-sergeant which too often is to be noticed in Prussia. More emphasis is laid on the individuality of the pupils than on a repetition of the words of the instructor. Thus if the pupils do not learn as much German literature by heart in the Saxon schools, they are better trained to appreciate its beauties. Literature is taught more systematically and the reading-book has been discarded for the masterpieces of German prose and poetry. And in the same way in the other subjects there is less memorizing and repetition and a greater interchange of activity between the teachers and the pupils. To one who visits the Saxon normal schools immediately after the Prussian the impression might almost be conveyed that there was a slackness in discipline, merely because of the military precision found in the latter. Into the scope of the subjects it is not necessary to enter,[16] inasmuch as they largely cover the same ground as in Prussia. Considerable time is given to Latin and at the end of the six years the pupils have a good command of the grammar and can read at sight with a certain amount of facility. Music is not compulsory in all its branches, but all pupils must learn singing. Two examinations are held in each class during the year, but promotions are made

---

[14]Gesetz über die Gymnasien, Realschulen und Seminare vom 22 Aug., 1876.

[15]Verordnung des Kult. Min. zur Ausführung des Gesetzes über die Gym., etc., vom 29 Jan., 1877.

[16]See Kretzschmar, J. F., p. 86 and pp. 352-379.

on the general standing for the whole year. The Saxon system has the advantage that the pupils have not to make new adjustments; the work is continuously maintained, the faculty has a better opportunity of knowing the pupils, and there is not the difficulty, which presents itself in Prussia, of pulling the pupils of the first year of the normal school together. One reform is mentioned as likely to take place within the next few years. It is very probable that an extra year will be added to the course and the age of admission will be reduced to thirteen and the first year will then be spent in securing a homogeneous class to begin the real work of the normal school in the second year. At Grimma a preparatory class has already been introduced unofficially. Whether this reform is in the right direction is an open question and the answer must depend upon the attitude which is taken up with regard to the system as it exists at present. But that the Saxon system compares very favorably with the Prussian there can be no doubt, and the advantage of Saxony comes almost entirely from the application of the methods of the secondary school and the grant of the rank of secondary schools to institutions which have to deal with boys over fourteen years of age. By this means a better class of teachers is secured and a spirit of scholarship is introduced.

In Bavaria[17] the same system of separate institutions for the preparation of pupils for the normal schools prevails as in Prussia, with the exception that the candidates must enter preparatory institution connected with the normal school to which they have been assigned. The preparatory institutions are under the charge of a principal and two assistant teachers. The principal receives his appointment from the King, the assistants, who are selected from elementary school teachers, from the Minister of the educational department. The assistants receive from 1860-2940 M. ($465-735) per year and have the privileges of state servants. The salary of the principal is the same as that of a normal school teacher. The preparatory institutions are inspected by the district inspectors and the director of the affiliated normal school. Higher authorities also have the right of inspection, but this is usually delegated. Candidates for entrance must be between 13-17 years of age and must be able to pass an examina-

---

[17]Englmann, pp. 144-158.

tion in the subjects of the seventh year of an elementary school. In the majority of the Bavarian preparatory institutions the pupils board and lodge in houses approved by the authorities. Support is given to deserving pupils in sums ranging from 52-120 M. a year. The curriculum differs from that of Prussia only in the time allotments for certain subjects. Religious instruction is given by the local pastor. A foreign language is not taught. A pupil's promotion depends on his work throughout the year, and at the end of the three years a leaving certificate is not given, but an examination for entrance into the normal school must be passed. It is proposed as soon as the means can be obtained to make the connection of the preparatory institutions with the normal schools more real than at present and to add a sixth year to the course.

But the question of what constitutes adequate preparation or what should be the appropriate institution for giving this preparation has not been settled in Germany, as may be seen in the reports of the proceedings of teachers' associations and other bodies interested in education. As at present constituted the system of preparatory training is based on a thoroughly German principle. Measuring qualifications by the amount and character of subject-matter covered instead of by intellectual efficiency, the authorities seem to have worked back from the goal to be attained, in this case the equipment of an elementary school teacher, and have organized their system accordingly. Hence comes the uniformity of prerequisites within each state and the single, definite course which all who wish to enter the teaching profession must follow. This principle prevails in all walks of life, giving rise to a narrow caste-system. The career of a boy is marked out for him by the school which he attends. But while the learned professions are numerous, the boy who begins his preparation for the normal school has nothing before him but the teaching profession. There is a strong division of opinion on this question. It is felt, on the one hand, that 14, the age at which preparation at present begins, is too early an age to make the choice of a profession; that this brings with it all the dangers of early specialization, narrowness, lack of sustained interest and routine methods; that the separation in institutions apart from boys destined for other professions is calculated to produce the same results. It is argued, on the other hand, by those who agree with Professor Rein[18] that the present system has advantages which compensate for these dangers. The specialized institution is necessarily small, hence the influence of the faculty can make itself better felt and a more uniform system can be maintained. Such instruction as will prepare directly for the normal school can be given to the exclusion of extraneous matter. No other type of school, for example, can give the requisite amount of religious or musical training. In the gymnasium too much attention is given to the ancient languages for which the elementary school teacher will have little use. In the modern schools science and languages are taught to a greater extent than will be required in the normal schools and too little attention is paid to the mother tongue, which is of the highest importance to the future teacher of the people. Lastly, to admit pupils from different types of schools with a variety of training would lead to difficulties of organization in the normal schools.

A reform of the system is at present proposed which should bring the preparatory institutions into line with the other high schools. While it is thought that these do not give either the right kind or the right amount of instruction in the subjects which are thought desirable for an elementary school teacher, the force of the objection that there is danger in the separation which at present exists is being recognized. It is now proposed that instead of allowing candidates to prepare in any secondary school in order to reap the advantages of associating with boys looking to other professions, the preparatory institutions should be extended by a year and should admit pupils who do not propose to enter normal schools. Such schools would correspond in a measure to higher elementary or middle schools and would include a foreign language in the curriculum. Such a system would, however, only meet with success in small towns removed from the competition of a secondary school and the prestige accompanying it. At the same time Rein[19] suggests that pupils from the *Real* and *Oberrealschule* should be permitted to enter the normal schools, receiving full credit for the standard which they have attained.

---

[18]Rein, Zur Reform der Lehrerbildung. *Jahrbuch des Vereins für wissenschaftliche Pädagogik.* (Dresden, 1902.)

[19]Ibid., *Der deutsche Schulmann,* 1902.

The general course, however, would be to attend the specialized school, which would stand in the same relation to the normal school as the gymnasium to the university or the *Oberrealschule* to the technical high school. This proposal, though perhaps not meeting the views of the teaching body as a whole, which would prefer to allow the preparation to be made in any type of school, has been supported by other educationalists of experience.[20] But whatever the theoretical opinion on the subject may be, it is highly probable that the present system will be retained in practice. An additional year may be introduced into the course, or some modifications may be made in the curriculum, but the training of teachers will continue to be given in institutions separated from the general school system.

---

[20]E.g. Seyfert, Vorschläge zur Reform der Lehrerbildung (Leipzig, 1905); Schmidt, A. M., in Mitteilungen des Vereins der Freunde Herbartischer Pädagogik in Thüringen (Langensalza, 1907).

CHAPTER IV

THE NORMAL SCHOOLS (VOLKSSCHULLEHRER-SEMINARIEN)

The training of teachers in Germany is entirely a matter of state control. Each state has its own system and maintains uniformity within its own territory. Although provision is made, for example, in Prussia for the examination of candidates for school appointments who have not been trained in a normal school, such cases very rarely occur.[1] The only instance where private preparation is recognized in Prussia is in the training of female teachers, but the next few years will probably see a change in this practice. But even in this case the normal schools are guided by the requirements for the government examination and, as already mentioned, by the regulations for the state normal school for women at Droyssig.[2] In Saxony there also exist provisions for the examination of extern candidates, but very few avail themselves of these. An exception is, however, made in the case of those who have passed the examination for appointment in a higher school at the University of Leipzig and in the case of candidates for the ministry. The former are eligible at once for permanent appointment in an elementary school, the latter only after passing the regular second examination.[3] Regulations for the female normal schools were included in the general law of 1876 for gymnasiums, real schools and normal schools.[4]

The Prussian authorities recognize the temporary appointment of teachers who have obtained their training and qualifications in some other German state, provided only that they pass the second examination for permanent appointment in due course.[5] Foreign-

[1]Bremen, p. 265.
[2]See Ch. I; *Central-Blatt*, 1892, p. 414.
[3]Seydewitz, pp. 62, 63.
[4]Kretzschmar, J. F., pp. 92-100.
[5]Bremen, p. 368.

ers must obtain the approval of the Minister before they can be permitted to teach in a German school, although by a decree of 1885 women teachers trained within the state are to be preferred. More liberality is shown in the inter-state recognition without further examination of women teachers than of men.[6] In Saxony candidates who have obtained the qualifications for temporary appointment outside the state must in each case receive the approval of the Minister before they can be appointed, and must undertake to present themselves for the examination for permanent appointment (*Wahlfähigkeitsprüfung*).[7]

The normal schools in Prussia are under the direct supervision of the Provincial School Boards and are maintained almost wholly at the expense of the state. The pupils pay no fees but must pay for their board, which amounts on an average to about one mark (25c.) a day. Slightly more than two-fifths of the students board in the normal schools.[8] The teachers find a cause for grievance against the boarding system, seeing in it another attempt to curb their independence. Since the majority of the preparatory institutions are not boarding-schools, many of the pupils are brought under the rigid discipline of the *Internat* for the first time, when they have reached the age of seventeen, and should be trained in habits of independence and self-direction. And the discipline of the normal school is indeed rigorous. The work of every hour of the day is definitely mapped out in the daily ordinances of each school (*Tagesordnung*).[9] Instead of being brought into contact with the world in which in some measure they are to be leaders, the normal school pupils are carefully withdrawn from it. Free organizations and societies among the pupils are unknown or are very rare. Athletics are gradually being introduced but have not the approval of the authorities, who have pinned their faith in gymnastics and organized physical training. Nor is the accommodation at all elaborate. The dormitories contain from twenty to ninety beds and are not always very well ventilated. The study-rooms are shared by six to eight boys and contain nothing but a large table and chairs. The walls are in most cases bare of pictures and the idea of alumni presentations has not yet been intro-

[6] Ibid., pp. 360-362.
[7] Seydewitz, p. 62.
[8] *Central-Blatt*, 1909, p. 780.
[9] See appendix.

duced. In respect of food the pupils have nothing to complain of, and good substantial fare is provided. The internal arrangements of the normal schools in Prussia are contracted out to a steward (*Oekonom*), who usually finds this a profitable undertaking. On the whole, however, one cannot resist the feeling that there is something military or monastic about the system. Instances of genuine personal friendship between an instructor and pupils are rarely met with. The instructor is in every case in the position of a superior and the pupils must keep their distance. That there are exceptions goes without saying and in this connection it may be mentioned that a new type of director is gradually being introduced, who is acquainted with schools and institutions different from the normal schools. Very often the martinet belongs to the period of 1872 and received his training under the influence of the reaction. There is no doubt that when this type is superseded a freer atmosphere will be found in the normal schools. But the boarding system is a survival of the reactionary and clerical influence. At present it is justified on the grounds that the pupils receive better accommodation at the price which they are paying, than they could obtain by boarding with private families. On the other hand the system of permitting the pupils to board in approved homes is found very satisfactory in a normal school not very far from Berlin, although even here the spirit of distrust is retained and the instructors must make tours of inspection every evening. But nothing can make up for the influence and surroundings of the home, nor is there any attempt to provide anything to replace these.

Just as the retention of the boarding system is due to the early clerical influence, so the location of normal schools in Prussia in small towns is due to the political reaction of 1848. A suspicion then engendered that the teachers were taking too much part in politics and were otherwise indulging in too high aspirations led to the banishment of the normal schools from the larger towns. In this way the pupils are deprived of the beneficial influences of the large town, such as museums, libraries, concerts and theatres. And the same policy has also a narrowing influence on the instructors. In this way the elementary school teachers, who in most cases are drawn from the country and must hold their first appointment in a rural school, are deprived of an experience which could not fail to be educative. This policy will, however, continue to be maintained. As an instance may be quoted the fact that the Normal School for Training City School Teachers (*Seminar für Stadtschullehrer*) is being removed from Berlin to a suburb. It is interesting to notice that the normal schools for women teachers are attached to large secondary schools for girls, are extern and are situated in the larger towns.

Buildings and equipment for normal schools are provided by the state. By a decree of 1864 land for such buildings must be given free by the communities.[10] Until recently the buildings conformed to one general plan; they were rather long, were built of red brick and had two projecting wings. More recent structures, however, display more individuality and are architecturally more ambitious. The following is the usual equipment of a Prussian normal school:[11]

1. Two or three class-rooms, each to accommodate thirty pupils.
2. A large class-room to accommodate two classes together.
3. An assembly-room, containing an organ.
4. Several music rooms, containing organs and pianos.
5. A practice-school with class-rooms large enough to admit the presence of a few students.
6. A drawing-room.
7. A class-room for instruction in physics and chemistry with seats arranged in tiers and with a table for performing experiments and cabinets for apparatus, etc.
8. A library.
9. A gymnasium.
10. A large garden.

Such is the general equipment of the normal schools. But the majority of the buildings are antiquated, so that it would be unjust to pass any criticism on them. Suffice it to say that generally the class-rooms are badly ventilated and lighted, that in many cases the ceilings are almost black, that the drawing-rooms are inadequately lighted, and that the science rooms contain but the one table on which the instructors alone can perform experiments. The apparatus for physics and the chemical supplies are always kept in the one room often to the detriment of the former. Sup-

[10]Bremen, p. 280.
[11]Ibid., pp. 280-281.

plies depend on the request of the instructors but there is neither haste nor generosity in meeting the demands. The seating accommodation in the class-rooms is very poor. Individual desks are unknown. Usually the pupils sit at long desks, six in a row, and frequently, when a pupil is called out to the board, he must climb over the others in his row. The organs, of which there are generally three in each normal school, and the pianos represent the largest item in the expenditure. The organ and music rooms are by no means sound-proof and, as pupils are practising throughout the day, there is always some accompaniment to the work of the class-rooms. Apart from the most necessary equipment the class-rooms are very barely furnished, and if they contain any pictures at all, these are of a religious character or are portraits of members of the reigning house. An exception must be made in favor of the assembly-halls (*Aula*), which are frequently adorned with valuable frescoes. The most pleasing part in the equipment of a normal school is the garden, which is well kept by the pupils.

The faculty of a Prussian normal school consists of the director, a chief assistant (*Oberseminarlehrer*) and five or six ordinary assistants (*ordentliche Seminarlehrer*). Great care is exercised in their selection, not only because their work differs from that of other teachers in so far as they have different material and different aims to deal with, but also because they have the responsibility of training teachers who in turn are to bring up a people loyal to the established order of government, as was pointed out in a letter sent by the Kaiser and Bismarck to the Ministry in 1890.[12] The requirements for appointment in the normal schools are very strictly laid down in theory, but are frequently departed from in the appointment of the director. All candidates must have passed the ordinary examinations for elementary school teachers and in addition the examinations for appointment in an intermediate school (*Mittelschule*) and as principals of elementary schools.[13] Thus the majority of candidates are men who have been trained in the normal schools originally and after that course have educated themselves. Two implications follow from this—that the old traditions of the normal schools are perpetuated, and the instructors have the defects of self-educated men, a cer-

[12]Bremen, p. 230.
[13]Ibid., p. 267, and Ch. VIII.

tain narrowness and inclination to dogmatism. A new type of normal school instructors is at present being introduced in rapidly increasing numbers. These are men who have had a university education and have passed the examination for appointment as teachers in secondary schools (*Oberlehrerexamen*). They must further pass the examination for appointment as principals of elementary schools. If they have not taught before, they are employed for a year in a normal school at a very small salary, not more than 100 M. a month, in order to make themselves acquainted with the work (*informatorische Beschäftigung*). At the end of this period they are appointed on probation for three months. The university trained men are singled out very soon for the positions of chief assistants, from which they may look forward to promotion as directors of normal schools or as district school inspectors. Without dwelling on the question of the injustice done to older men by the rapid advancement of the young university graduate, there can be no doubt that the new policy will infuse much needed reform in the traditional groove into which the normal schools have fallen, provided always that a careful selection is made to secure men who have a genuine interest in the elementary schools and in the training of teachers for these schools. At present the majority of the normal school teachers are normal school graduates, while the chief assistants are equally divided between normal school and university graduates. The directors are, with the exception of only sixteen cases, university graduates. An enquiry made in 1900 showed that of 118 directors 63 or 53 per cent. had taken a theological and 30 a literary course at the university.[14]

The question of the best preparation for normal school instructors is still a matter of debate in Prussia. While it is recognized that the appointment of normal school graduates would lead to the dangers of inbreeding, it is at the same time admitted that while university graduates would help to raise the standards, the universities do not at present afford a satisfactory training in pedagogy and the allied subjects as a preparation for school work. The best course would be to combine a training at the normal schools with some training at the universities. It should be pointed out, however, that graduation from a normal school is not

[14]*Rept. U. S. Com. Educ.*,1900, p. 202.

considered as a fulfillment of the requirements for entrance into a Prussian university, although normal school graduates may enter as auditors.[15]

For the present the training of normal school teachers at the universities is impossible. The government, however, has arranged a special course since 1897 for this purpose in Berlin.[16] Provision is made for thirty students who are drawn from the ranks of middle school, preparatory and normal school teachers, school inspectors and young university graduates. These are recommended by the County and Provincial School Boards to the attention of the ministry, owing to special merit. They must bind themselves by an agreement to serve in a normal school for eight years after completing the course. There are no fees to pay and the state gives bursaries of 125 M. per month for maintenance.[17] The length of the course has not yet been definitely settled and it has varied from its institution from one to two years. At present its duration is one year, and this will very shortly be extended to eighteen months. The course is mainly academic, but in addition to lectures includes visits to museums, art collections and educational institutions. The lectures are given by some of the most prominent professors and scholars to be found in Berlin. The students may also attend lectures at the university as auditors. The following subjects are obligatory on all students: (1) pedagogy and philosophy, (2) German language and literature, (3) history of art and civilization, (4) hygiene, (5) economics. In addition there are optional courses in mathematics, geography, physics, chemistry, zoology, physiology of speech, history, English and French, and social economics (*Wohlfahrtskunde*). Besides affording a training in the academic subjects the course further aims at instructing the students in the spirit of the regulations and decrees issued by the ministry. There is an inclination on the part of those who have taken the course to criticize it because there is no provision for a final examination and some diploma or a degree, as a spur to continued effort during its

---

[15]Lexis, Vol. III, pp. 248-254; *Pädagogisches Jahrbuch*, 1907, p. 207; Schöppa, G., Die Bestimmungen des Königlich preussischen Ministers der geistlichen, Unterrichts-und Medizinalangelegenheiten (Leipzig, 1909), p. 135.

[16]Lexis, p. 251.

[17]*Central-Blatt*, 1898, p. 714.

short duration. Petty though this criticism is, it would not have been found necessary to mention it, had it not been raised by several teachers. A more important objection is that the course is entirely academic and to that extent divorced from the practice of the class-room. In general, however, there is an inclination on the part of elementary and normal school teachers to view the course with suspicion as a mere subterfuge on the part of the government to delay their admission to the universities.

Another practice[18] which also serves as a means for the training of normal school instructors is to visit other normal schools. Once in five years an instructor in a normal school may obtain leave of absence for fourteen days for the purpose of visiting from three to four normal schools. The expenses of travelling are borne by the state. The aim is to obtain an acquaintance with practice in different parts of the country. In practice, however, the system does not justify itself, because of the uniformity throughout the state which does not afford a sufficient variety of experience. But the suggestion contained in the practice is valuable. A report of the work seen without any criticism must be sent to the Ministry.

There are further courses for the preparation of specialist teachers in music, drawing and gymnastics. Teachers of music receive their training at the Academical Institute for church music,[19] which also undertakes the training of organists, choir-leaders and cantors. The course, which is open to candidates of musical ability who have already passed the first examination for elementary school teachers, extends over eighteen months and includes instruction in the playing of the organ, piano, and violin, singing, harmony, and counterpoint. The number of students admitted to each course is limited to twenty, and permission to sit for the entrance examination is at the discretion of the Minister. Candidates pay no fees, but must maintain themselves at their own expense during their stay in Berlin. There is no final examination, but each student receives a certificate endorsed by the members of the faculty setting forth the qualifications shown for work in any of the branches for which the Institute prepares.

Special courses for teachers of drawing are offered by a number of schools of art, the most important of which is the Royal

---

[18]Lexis, Vol. III, p. 253.
[19]Schöppa, pp. 126-129.

School of Art in Berlin.[20] Candidates, who must already be in service, are admitted to the examination for entrance into any of these schools on the presentation of some original work of art. The course lasts for two years and those who desire to become teachers of drawing in graded elementary, middle, secondary and normal schools, must pass a state examination. Besides the ordinary branches of drawing and painting there are also tests on the history of art and method. The candidates receive certificates showing their qualifications to teach drawing either in the lower or the higher schools.[21]

For those who wish to specialize in the teaching of gymnastics a course is offered centrally at the Royal Training Institution for Teachers of Gymnastics in Berlin.[22] Facilities are also afforded in other towns. Candidates must be medically fit and must pass a number of tests in gymnastics before they are admitted. There are no fees to be paid and in some cases the state gives small allowances for maintenance. The duration of the course is one year and preparation is given for the state examination for teachers of gymnastics,[23] which is based on a knowledge of the theory of physical exercise, anatomy, hygiene and first aid to the injured, as well as ability to perform exercises and to teach the subject. The successful candidates receive appointments in schools for which they already have qualifications.

The division of the instructors into directors, chief assistants, and ordinary assistants has already been mentioned. There seems to be no principle underlying the appointment of the chief assistants (*Oberlehrer*). It may be due either to private influence or to merit. At present the tendency is to appoint young men who have had an academic training and show promise of becoming the future administrators of the state. There is a distinction in the salaries according to these three grades. The directors receive from 4000-6600 M. ($1000-1650) ; chief assistants 3000-4800 M. ($750-1200) ; ordinary assistants 2400-4200 M. ($600-1050). To these sums must of course be added a free house or compensation for rent, the use of a part of the garden frequently attached to a normal school, and the right to a pension.

---

[20]Schöppa, p. 136.
[21]Ibid., pp. 182-188.
[22]Ibid, pp. 131.134.
[23]Ibid., pp. 177-182.

The number of pupils in a normal school is usually ninety, or thirty to a class. The cases of variation from this number are not frequent. When the demand for teachers becomes very pressing, extra classes are established. It is difficult to make any generalization about the grades of society from which the pupils are drawn. Formerly the majority were the sons of farmers or farm laborers. At present the tendency seems to be in the direction of an increase in the number of sons of civil and municipal servants of lower rank to enter the teaching profession. A few tables will be given for the sake of comparison, although this task is made difficult by the differences in classification and grouping.[24]

PRUSSIA

PARENTS' OCCUPATION	PERCENTAGE OF TEACHERS	
	1906	1901
Agriculture and gardening.......................	32.86	33.55
Mining, manufacture and building................	26.87	27.40
Trade and commerce............................	12.10	11.18
Servants and day laborers.......................	.68	.64
Civil and municipal servants and professions (including teachers)................................	23.17	22.70
Without calling.................................	4.40	4.53

The percentage of those whose parents were teachers in elementary and middle schools was 17.73 in 1906 as against 18.90 in 1901, showing a decrease which was probably due to the agitation among teachers for an increase in salary.

A table of 1906 for the Duchy of Gotha[25] shows that of the teachers 67.34 per cent. came from the country districts and 32.66 per cent. from towns. According to the occupation of their parents they were divided as follows:

PARENTS' OCCUPATION	PERCENTAGE
Trade and commerce....................................	40.70
Agriculture...	33.88
Civil and municipal servants and professions (including teachers, 13.30 per cent.)...	23.73
Artisans..	1.45
Without calling..	1.24

[24]*Pädagogisches Jahrbuch*, 1907, p. 177.

[25]Ibid., 1906, p. 117.

For Saxony[26] the following table from a normal school with two hundred and forty pupils may be taken as representative of the classes of society from which the future members of the teaching profession are recruited:

Parents' Occupation	Percentage
Trade and commerce	32.10
Agriculture and gardening	6.66
Civil and municipal servants (including teachers, 12.50 per cent.)	30.83
Artisans	29.16
Without occupation	1.25

The marked differences between Prussia and Saxony can be accounted for not only by the fact that the one country is predominantly agricultural, while the other is chiefly industrial, but also because the salaries paid in Saxony were until recently far higher than those paid in Prussia. A striking feature of both tables is the small proportion of pupils who are the sons of teachers. It is generally admitted, however, in Germany that the sons of teachers usually attain to a rank in life above that of their parents.

But however varied the origin of the pupils the rigorous discipline of the preparatory institutions and the normal schools reduces them to uniformity. No encouragement is given to cultivate individual tastes. And indeed the long working day makes outside activities almost impossible. In some normal schools opportunities for free associations in charge of an instructor are given. These take the form of chess clubs, scientific societies and clubs along other lines of interest, and meet once a week, usually on Sundays. But debating, glee, orchestral, literary societies are not usual. Such time as can be spared the pupils employ in lounging round the towns, making purchases or in walking. For general reading there does not seem to be either the necessary time or facilities. Although every normal school has a library, it is usually stocked with old text-books. The arrangements for the use of the libraries vary. In some schools the library is open once a month for the exchange of books; in others once in two weeks. In no case does the pupils have access to the shelves. The library is in charge of one of the instructors, assisted by a pupil. It is said that the pupils do not read much outside their school work, because they already have enough to read in connection with the

---

[26]Based on the returns of the parents' occupations given in the register of a normal school in Saxony.

literary course. But as the time-tables and the libraries are organized at present no encouragement is offered to the pupils to pursue general reading.

There are two half holidays each week and these are employed in taking longer walks, if not in making up the class-work. Once a month there is a whole holiday in which the pupils must revise such of the work as they are backward in or have missed in class.

The supervision of the students outside the class-rooms is taken in turns by the instructors. A measure of responsibility is delegated to the senior student of the school, who acts as the intermediary between the director and the pupils, and to the senior students of the study-rooms. It is the duty of these to maintain order in their respective rooms and to appoint some pupil· to keep the room clean and tidy. Further there are class-room and other monitors, and the general scheme makes for a mechanical performance of the daily round. A scale of penalties or punishments does not exist because it is not necessary. A word of censure is sufficient to cow the oldest pupil into obedience. A report to the director might easily be fraught with serious consequences. Hence there is an almost painful orderliness and quiet about the normal schools even during free periods.

The broad features of the Prussian normal schools are reproduced in Saxony, and yet there is a marked difference between the two. The Saxon schools seem to be devoid of that system of mechanical routine, of that suppression of the individual which are so marked in Prussia. The Saxon normal schools are of course larger, since they have twice the number of classes, but the effects of discipline are not so oppressively felt. The reason for the difference has already been suggested.

The number of the members on the faculty of a normal school in Saxony is not fixed. According to the law of 1876 up to one-third of the instructors must be elementary school teachers without academic qualifications.[27] These should be appointed to give the practical training and to teach in the practice school. Apart from the specialist teachers in drawing and music the rest of the instructors are men with academic training who have passed the examination for appointment in a higher school or the pedagogical examination at the University of Leipzig. The former examina-

[27]Kretzschmar, J. F., p. 89.

tion[28] is held before a royal examining commission. It is both written and oral and extends over academic and professional subjects. All candidates must pass in philosophy, pedagogy, German literature and religion. The professional subjects are those which the candidate expects to teach in a higher school. Three subjects must be selected from the following: Christian religion, elements of philosophy, German, Latin, Greek, French, English, history, geography, pure mathematics, applied mathematics, physics, chemistry, mineralogy, botany and zoology. In addition three theses must be prepared and a model lesson in some subject selected by the candidate must be presented before the examiners.

Those, however, who only wish to obtain the qualifications to teach in a normal or Real school, may do so by passing the pedagogical examination at the University of Leipzig.[29] The examining commission is appointed by the Minister of Culture and Education. The subjects of the examination are, with the exception that Greek and the elements of philosophy are not included, the same as in the examination for candidates for the higher schools. Only two theses are demanded, one of which must be on some pedagogical subject. The model lesson may at the discretion of the examiners be presented in an elementary or higher school or in both. The examination in the subjects which the candidate hopes to teach is not of such a wide scope as in the examination for the teachers in the higher schools.

All candidates irrespective of the examination which they have passed must serve a year's probation in a school to which they have been assigned by the Ministry. During this year they are not expected to give more than six hours' instruction during the week.[30]

Until definitely appointed the salaries[31] of normal school instructors range from 1200-2100 M. ($300-520) per year besides a house, heat and light and the expectation of a pension. The permanently appointed teachers receive from 2400-6000 M. ($600-1500) per year. The directors' salaries begin at 6000 M. ($1500) and rise to 6600 M. ($1650) per year. A scale of compensation for

[28]Ibid., pp. 498-522.
[29]Ibid., pp. 524-536.
[30]Ibid., p. 37.
[31]Ibid., pp. 585-6.

rent[32] was drawn up in 1902 for the civil servants of Saxony and the normal school instructors come under its provisions. In each school-building provision is made for housing the director and one assistant instructor, who has charge of the students after school hours.

As in Prussia there is a distinction into ordinary and chief assistants. The distinction in salary, however, does not prevail. Complaints are heard here also that the older men are passed over in favor of younger men with academic training in the award of the title of chief assistant (*Oberlehrer*). There may be several instructors in each school with this title. One of these is designated as the first chief assistant, and in case of need he represents the director. Another title given to instructors in normal as well as other higher schools is that of "Professor," granted only to those who have completed a long and meritorious period of service.

A few points of detail may be mentioned in which the administration of a Saxon normal school differs from the Prussian. Each class is assigned to one instructor who has charge of that group for a whole year. Of course the numbers necessitate some arrangement by which the pupils may feel that there is one instructor in particular whom they may consult, and to whom they are responsible for their work and conduct during the year. Not only are the pupils under the charge of one instructor, but cases of difficulty may be brought to the notice of the faculty at the meetings which must be held at least once a month to discuss the affairs of the school. In the matter of punishments for refractory pupils may be mentioned a survival of the punishment cell, which is not infrequently used. There is the same feeling as in Prussia that for purposes of discipline the small town is the best location for a normal school. The oldest Saxon normal school is about to be removed from the capital to a suburb.

Within the last few years there has been a rapid increase in the number of normal schools. At first these were called for by the dearth of teachers and were begun in the form of extra classes attached to existing normal schools at that time. As soon as buildings were put up to accommodate the new school, these extra classes were removed and formed the nucleus of an additional

---

[32]Ibid., pp. 586-590.

normal school. Although the supply of teachers has become normal recently, the extra courses were retained and still further additions to the number of normal schools are contemplated, in order to supply sufficient teachers to reduce the number of pupils in a class of the elementary schools of forty.

In Bavaria the normal schools have only a two years' course. Of the twelve normal schools all are boarding-schools. The pupils pay only for their food. Everything else is provided by the institution and support is given to the poorer boys. Generally the faculty consists of the director and two instructors, but these may be assisted by an assistant instructor or teachers who do not give their full time to the normal school. The director is appointed by the King with the approval of the Bishop of the diocese in which the school is located. If the director is not in holy orders, then the first instructor must be. He holds the title of "Prefect." Both instructors are appointed by the King, and where the director is in orders the instructors are selected from able elementary school teachers. In addition to a free house or the compensation for rent and the right to a pension the salaries of normal school instructors are as follows: The directors receive from 3720-4800 M. ($930-1200) per year. The other instructors receive from 2280-3360 M. ($570-840) per year. Where necessary the ministry may sanction the appointment of one or two assistant instructors at a salary of from 1500-1860 M. ($375-465) at the end of six years' service.[33]

No other qualifications are demanded from candidates for service in the normal schools than that they should have passed the second examination for permanent appointment in elementary schools. In 1900 the Ministry for education instituted a course for normal school instructors in mathematics and physics, and in 1901 in chemistry and mineralogy.[34] Both courses are held in Munich. Since the normal school course proper only extends over two years, the assistance of able elementary school teachers is employed for the training of candidates in the practical work of the school. On this part of Bavarian system more will be said later.

---

[33]Englmann, Handbuch des bayerischen Volksschulrechts, pp. 161-164.
[34]Lexis, Vol. III, p. 306.

Except for the fact that pupils are under the disciplinary authority of the normal school throughout the year, including vacations, the regulations for the internal working of the schools are similar to those found in the two other states, which have already been dealt with. With reference to the conduct of the pupils during the vacations,[35] the instructors at their discretion may ask a pupil to bring a certificate from the school authorities of the district where they spent the period.

---

[35]Englmann, p. 175.

CHAPTER V

THE NORMAL SCHOOL CURRICULUM. ACADEMIC SUBJECTS

The normal schools of Prussia and Bavaria are in the majority of cases institutions distinct from the preparatory departments. Although the two institutions nominally form a unit, the practice of imposing an entrance examination on candidates for the normal schools has survived. In Prussia, however, the leaving examination of a state preparatory department is recognized as an entrance qualification, while candidates who have had any other preparation must present themselves at the normal schools for examination. The two examinations, whether the final in a state preparatory department or entrance, are essentially the same, the only difference being in the constitution of the examining board. In the former the examiners consist of the instructors of the department,[1] a representative of the provincial school board and a director of a normal school of the province. The examining board in the latter case[2] includes the members of the normal school at which the examination is held, and a representative of the provincial school board. Entrance examinations are held once a year and only as many candidates as there is room for in the normal school are declared to have passed, although reports of the work of all candidates may be obtained by directors of other normal schools on application. Candidates must be between the ages of 17 and 24. Their application forms must be accompanied by certificates of baptism, vaccination and health, and a declaration of the parent or guardian of ability to maintain the candidate during his stay at the normal school. The only expense is for board, all else being provided, while the state, as was pointed out earlier, gives support in many cases. The examination is both

---

[1]Bremen, pp. 241-243.
[2]Ibid., pp. 256-259.

written and oral. The written test consists of an essay and questions on subjects of the preparatory department. Candidates who do unsatisfactory work in the written test may be excluded from the oral. All candidates must reach a satisfactory standard in religion, language, arithmetic, geometry, history, music and real subjects. Failure in any of these subjects serves to exclude the candidate. Tests are also given in a modern language, drawing and gymnastics. The greatest stress, however, is laid on religion, the mother-tongue and arithmetic. In the first of these subjects candidates are expected to know the language, history, moral and religious content of the whole Bible with a special knowledge of certain parts, the catechism and some twenty hymns. In German candidates are expected to have a knowledge of grammar, spelling and expressive reading, and must be able to recite a number of poems. Accuracy and facility in mental arithmetic and blackboard work in the most important arithmetical operations are demanded. Exceptionally high standards are set, and the marking is unnecessarily severe. The ordeal of the oral examination is very trying. Added to the social importance which is attached to examinations in Germany, and the natural nervousness of the candidates, the tone of a large number of examiners is not calculated to set the candidates at their ease or to contribute to any genuine test of real merit. Hence it is not surprising if at the oral tests candidates stumble over the simplest grammatical rules, or stammer through poems which they have repeated frequently in the elementary and preparatory schools. But a candidate must be endowed with a very minimum of ability to be rejected.

On passing the examination candidates must submit to an examination at the hands of the medical officer of the normal school. Another requirement before all the qualifications for entrance are complete is a signed declaration (*Revers*) of the candidate to return all sums paid to him for support during his stay in the normal school, and a fixed amount for the expenses of tuition, in the event of his leaving the normal school through ill-health or at the request of the authorities in the case of poor work, or in the event of refusing any appointment offered to him in the public school service by the provincial or central authorities. By this means a guarantee is obtained for a fair standard of work in the normal school, and for a supply of teachers at the call of the state.

In Bavaria[3] the examinations for entrance into the normal schools is held for all candidates in the preparatory departments. The subjects of examination are the same as in Prussia with the same stress on arithmetic, religion and the mother-tongue. Candidates who acquit themselves excellently in the written examination are exempt from the oral.

In Saxony the pupils are promoted into the section of the training schools which correspond to the Prussian normal schools in the ordinary course by passing the annual promotional examination and on general satisfactory work. Provision is made for the entrance of pupils who have attended other schools into any part of the normal schools on passing an examination in the subjects which are prerequisite for the classes for which they seem to be suitable. In this way candidates are obtained from the *Realschule* and usually enter on the course of the third year. In some normal schools students who enter from other schools are placed in special classes. Thus at Annaberg there are separate classes for the graduates of the Realschule (*Realschulabiturienten*).

The curriculum of the normal schools forms an organic whole with that of the preparatory departments of whatever type they may be. Just as the preparatory curriculum is built up on that of the elementary schools, so that of the normal schools presupposes the curriculum of the preparatory department. Two principles seem to underly the work of the normal schools. The one is due to the requirements of the future calling of the pupils, the other to a recognition that the teachers of a nation must be men of culture. On the one hand there is a tendency to limit the curriculum to a deeper and more intensive study of the elementary school subjects, on the other there is the danger of extending the curriculum not only until it becomes unwieldy but to a point where the risk of overburdening the pupils is great. The problem of attaining the happy mean is very complex and is by no means relieved by the necessity of including the purely professional training in the curriculum. The conditions in the German normal schools hardly contribute to a solution of the difficulty. The burden in all the normal schools seems far greater than it should be for boys in the adolescent period. The question, however, has formed the subject of discussion for some time. The most valuable contribution has

---

[3]Englmann, pp. 166 ff.

been that of Dr. R. Seyfert, who in his "Vorschläge zur Reform der Lehrerbildung "[4] has made some happy suggestions, which are perhaps of too radical a character to meet with acceptance in Germany. His proposal in the main is that the training of the teacher shall be extended to seven years. The first five years of this course should be devoted entirely to academic instruction, and the last two to the purely professional work and specialization in one or two of the academic subjects. The objection that if such a course were adopted the academic training could be satisfactorily given in any of the existing secondary schools, he meets with the argument that the training of the teacher requires an ideal different from that which prevails in the other schools. Leaving the details of Seyfert's proposals on one side, he has undoubtedly succeeded in dealing with a problem of the normal schools which is all-important.

The Prussian *Regulations* of 1901 met with the approval of the teachers on the ground that at last the academic and professional work were kept distinct. Until that date the underlying principle had been that the work of the elementary schools had the first claim on the attention of the pupils. Accordingly considerable emphasis was placed on the subjects of the elementary schools to the extent that the regulations provided that the methods of the elementary school should be employed in the class-room of the normal school. But while the latest regulations for normal schools have enriched the curriculum and separated the academic from the professional work, the separation has not been made in time, with the result that both are carried side by side. At the same time in order to relieve the pupils of the necessary burden which was imposed, some of the subjects, as mathematics, geography and nature study, were dropped from the course of the final year. How far this step succeeded in preventing the danger of overburdening may be seen from the time-table,[5] which is an adequate plea for a more strictly defined separation between academic and professional studies. The Saxon system is similar to that of Prussia in retaining the professional subjects for three years side by side with the academic. In Bavaria the theory and principles of education are taught in the two years of the course, while the practice work is done after candidates leave the normal school.

---

[4]Leipzig, 1905.
[5]See appendix.

The curriculum of the normal schools of Prussia is fully prescribed in the " Course of study and suggestions for its operation " (*Lehrpläne für Präparandenanstalten und Lehrerseminare, sowie methodische Anweisungen zu beiden Lehrpläne vom 1 Juli 1901*). The regulations received the approval and praise of teachers for their liberal tendencies, for their emphasis on the cultural aim and for their contribution to enrichment of the curriculum. And indeed the regulations merit all that can be said in their praise. While it would be impossible to disagree with the laudatory estimate contained in a book like that of Gerstenhauer (*Zur Würdigung der Lehrpläne,* etc.),[6] it is to be deplored that the practice of the normal schools does not correspond with the theoretical prescriptions. The force of thirty years' tradition established under the *Regulations* of 1872 has not been able to spend itself in the nine years during which the new regulations have been in operation. It will require at least a generation of teachers with different preparation to undo the evil effects of inbreeding and tradition, and to introduce the spirit of the new regulations.

The necessity of repetition will be avoided if before proceeding with the scope of the subjects of the curriculum, some prefatory remarks are made here on the method employed in the classrooms. Generalizations are always dangerous but the account here submitted seems to be based on sufficient observation to warrant the statement. While it is recognized that the subject-matter must involve its own method, there is no evidence that this theory is put into practice in the German schools. It follows almost as a corollary of this that there is no attempt to deal with the psychology of a subject, that is, to interpret the experience for which a subject stands from the genetic standpoint, or from the point of view of one who realizes the experience. Each branch of the curriculum is regarded as so much information which the pupils must absorb. Great as is the theoretical opposition to the method of drilling or drumming in (*einpauken*) a subject, this is the method which is only too frequently to be observed in the Prussian normal schools. There is a wearisome similarity in the presentation of the different subjects of the curriculum. Every lesson begins with a short review, as no doubt it should, but there is too

---

[6]Gerstenhauer, Zur Würdigung der Lehrpläne, etc. (Breslau, 1906.)

much insistence on accurate verbal repetition and reproduction of the instructor's statement at the previous lesson. The remainder of the lesson consists not of development by an interchange of thought and activity between the instructor and the class, but of brief lectures by the instructor, followed by questions on each section and then more reproduction by the class. For a pupil to ask a question is a rare procedure to be attempted only with an indulgent instructor. Frequently the reproductions of the brief lectures are made in response to a command to "hold forth" (*vortragen*) on what has already been done and not to answer some question and, when one pupil has finished, the next is requested to continue (*fortsetzen*) where he left off. The pupil who is reciting monopolizes the whole of the instructor's attention. So well does the method here described cultivate the secondary attention, that a pupil who is obviously inattentive can rise to his feet, when called upon, and continue. The effect of this method, which will easily be recognized as a type of Herbartianism with the good points omitted, is that the students employ it in the practice-teaching, even to the extent of reproducing in the afternoon a lesson which they had themselves learned in the morning.

The pupils are not permitted to take notes of the lectures in most cases, and the text-books which are employed are intended to supplement the class-work. But the insistence on accurate reproduction is so strong, that means are found of taking notes somehow. In one school where an instructor carries the method so far that he scolds if a conjunction is omitted, the treasured property of one class consists of surreptitious notes on psychology which show that the instructor has not varied one word within seven years. As another illustration of the prevailing system the advice of an instructor to a graduating class on how to prepare for the examination in pedagogy in the Second Teachers Examination may be mentioned. He recommended the selection of a good text-book and then the learning of each new chapter of the book was to be accompanied by a repetition of all that had preceded it.

One feature of class-room procedure cannot be too highly recommended. Every instructor, no matter what his subject may be, insists on careful expression and accentuation. No occasion is omitted to remind the pupils that "speech is the most important instrument of the teacher," that "speech is the teacher's tool," and that "careful attention must be given to expression."

If the function of education in Germany is to produce "the God-fearing, patriotic, self-supporting citizen," the aim of the normal schools is to produce the teachers to carry out these ideals. The official "Course of study and suggestions" emphasize the ethical and character-building elements and the training for loyalty and patriotism. At the same time the emphasis which is laid on these ideals for the normal schools is avowedly with a view to the efficiency of the teacher in the elementary schools. The teacher is not merely to impart information to the youth of the country but to serve as an example of reverence and patriotism. Hence greater stress is put in the normal schools on those subjects which are regarded as fundamental for the elementary schools. The aim of the elementary school is declared to be the "religious, moral and national training, and knowledge and ability necessary for citizenship."[7] Accordingly an important place is assigned to religion, the mother-tongue, and mathematics, while the other subjects are only treated in their elements. The pupil who leaves the elementary school at the age of fourteen is expected to have a good knowledge of the story of the Bible and a special knowledge of the more important parts which are fundamental to the Christian faith, some acquaintance with the history of the church, the ability to recite some simple prayers and a number of hymns. In the mother tongue he will be expected to read with intelligence and expression, to spell, to have sufficient command of the language to express himself intelligently, and to have received an introduction to the best that there is in the literature of his nation. The national sense is to be quickened and to find its expression in an intense loyalty to the reigning house, as the embodiment of national greatness. In arithmetic it is expected that on leaving the elementary school a pupil will have acquired facility in accurate use of figures, including fractions, decimals, and the ordinary numerical processes which enter into daily life. A little geography, also with a national emphasis, drawing and some nature study will also be included in the training received in the elementary school.

The fundamentals of the elementary school as here described form the framework around which the curriculum of the normal

---

[7]Stötzner, Das öffentliche Unterrichtswesen Deutschlands, p. 9 (Leipzig, 1901).

school is built up. The demands of the elementary school enter more largely into the work of the normal schools than the importance of raising the intellectual level of the teaching profession.[8]

In religious instruction the scope is the same as in the secondary schools.[9] Three hours a week are given to the subject in the normal schools, as against two in the gymnasium. The normal school pupils cover much the same ground as in the elementary schools with a more intensive treatment and a more complete study of the history of the church. The present constitution of the evangelical church and the regulations for church services are added. There is a tendency to sacrifice the spiritual side to the informational. There appears to be very little disposition to question either the need or the extent of religious instruction in the normal schools, although voices are beginning to be raised here and there against the amount which is memorized.

There is a strong resemblance between the courses in German in the gymnasium[10] and the normal school. The same purpose underlies both, to give the pupils ability in the use of the language, an acquaintance with the masterpieces of literature and literary history, and a stronger feeling of patriotism. Instruction in grammar has been completed in the preparatory department and is only reviewed as occasion demands. Some attention is given to phonetics in order to enable the future teachers to cope with dialectical peculiarities. Good composition, written and oral, is insisted upon by all instructors, and in addition to regular class exercises two essays are usually written each month on a subject connected with the curriculum. The readings in literature of the third year would compare with those of *Unterprima* in extent. In addition to a wide selection of poetry six dramatical works, including a play of Shakespere, are prescribed for the three years. History of German literature is taught in connection with the readings of the class, supplemented by biographical sketches of important writers. To the class readings must be added private readings on which tests are given. In the teaching of literature too much attention is paid to form and content and too little to literary appreciation and judgment. The method of approach in

---

[8]For the curriculum see Schöppa, pp. 82-126.
[9]Consult Russell, German Higher Schools, Ch. XI.
[10]Ibid., Ch. XII.

the treatment of poems is to analyze and break them up into sections (*Zergliederung*), rarely to read them through as a whole. In dealing with dramatic works no attempt is made to realize them through action, although considerable attention is paid to the plot and in some cases to the psychological development of character. In view of the rapid inroads made by writings of the type of the "dime novel" (*Schundliteratur*), and in passing it may be said that many are translations of American detective and wild West stories, the pupils before leaving the normal schools are expected to obtain a knowledge of good popular and children's literature.

On the teaching of modern languages nothing need be added to what has already been said on the subject in preparatory departments. No useful purpose is served by the retention of the lessons as at present given. There is little interest either on the part of teacher or taught. The aim of the course in a modern language, which may be French or English, is ability to read easy pieces and familiarity with the grammar and syntax.

The teaching of history is a good illustration of the emphasis which is placed on one section of the "Methodical Suggestions" on the subject to the neglect of the rest. While these recommend that attention should be paid to historical criticism and the tracing of cause and effect together with the dependence of the present on the past, there is a strong tendency in the class-room to insist on a knowledge of dates and facts. The pupils are not encouraged to exercise independent judgment but to know the number of pages in the textbook which has been assigned. The greatest importance is naturally attached to the study of Prussian and then of German history. General European history is only introduced so far as it is required to illustrate the German. As the educators of the future citizens of the country the pupils in the normal schools are taught to understand the development and relations to each other of the different classes of society, and above all the services of the reigning house for the welfare of the people, for the Prussian schoolmaster is not only to be the teacher of youth but to act as a political bulwark against that evil which seems to the German to contradict all the ideas of historical development— social democracy.[11] Although the use of source material is pre-

---

[11]Schöppa, p. 48.

scribed, this was not much in evidence, and where it was employed, it was mainly as a picturesque supplement to the biographical element rather than for critical investigation. One instructor, a university graduate and specialist in the subject, stated that it was better not to use source material, since sufficient time could not be afforded for a proper study. He contented himself in the class-room with insisting on dates and facts (*einfach die Tatsache*).

Of the scientific group of subjects the greatest amount of time is given to mathematics. Excellent instruction is given in this subject. The work does not resolve itself merely into the solution of problems, but a strong emphasis is placed on logical thoroughness. In all the branches importance is attached to oral work, and facility in mental calculation. The problems are closely related to the needs of commerce and industry. A close and obvious relationship is maintained between arithmetic and algebra. In geometry the scope of the subject includes a familiarity with the commonest formulas. An introduction is given to trigonometry up to the use of logarithms and the solution of triangles. Throughout there is constant practice in working on the blackboard.

While geography in the gymnasium is taught in connection with history, in the normal schools the scientific aspect is emphasized. After a treatment of the mathematical and physical facts, attention is devoted to the relation of these to men's activities. A study of the geography of the world is followed by an intensive treatment of German and within recent years, of the colonial expansion. Some practice is given in the study of map-drawing in books as well as on the board, though the latter is necessarily limited by an inadequate equipment.

The elements of light and electricity form the scope of the teaching of physics, while chemistry includes the principles and some acquaintance with chief minerals and metals. The laboratory method is not as yet introduced, and instruction is in the form of lectures on experiments performed by the teacher. Opportunity is occasionally offered after school hours for students to make experiments. In the majority of the normal schools agriculture still forms a branch of the curriculum. The large gardens which are attached to most of the schools are used for practical work in vegetable growing and the culture of fruit-trees. Since the teachers in the majority of cases hold their first appointments in agricultural communities, this study is of great importance to them as leaders, and practically it is of benefit to them in the management of the school and their own private gardens.

The subjects of the scientific group are brought to a conclusion at the end of the second year. In the last year the method of teaching each of them is given.

A disproportionate amount of time is devoted to the study and practice of music. Although pupils without ability may be excused from learning harmony and the organ, very few avail themselves of exemption. Singing and violin playing are compulsory for all. While much attention is given to the formal and technical branches, the execution rarely attains a satisfactory standard. The violin, which is admittedly a difficult instrument to play, is retained as a cheap portable instrument for the use of teachers in giving instruction in singing in the elementary schools. The extent of the instruction in this subject is accounted for by the necessity of preparing teachers for appointments which are connected with the position of organists and choirleaders.

The teaching of drawing is generally admitted to be indebted to the works of American writers, such as Liberty Tadd and the publications of Prang. The chief emphasis is placed on practice, while theoretical and formal instruction is kept in the background. Excellent work is done in drawing from models and nature. Although the equipment as well as the class-rooms is poor, the teachers, who in all cases are specialists, show considerable ingenuity in the collection of suitable models, and in providing their pupils with opportunities of sketching and painting from nature. While a certain amount of correlation with other subjects of the curriculum is required by the regulations, the teachers of drawing jealously guard against dictation on this score. The teaching of perspective is the only branch of this subject which receives much formal treatment. Owing to the limitation already mentioned blackboard drawing can receive very little of the attention which the regulations consider desirable.

What the English schools strive to attain through athletics, the German schools aim at by means of organized gymnastics. But while English athletics are largely a matter of individual choice, gymnastics in Germany are permeated with national aims and have a political tradition of almost a century behind them. Physical welfare, determination, endurance, self-control and the subordination of the individual to the group are among the aims of instruction in gymnastics.) Without entering into the merits of athletics over against gymnastics it may be mentioned that a gradual change is making itself felt in the attitude of the Germans to the subject, and more attention is being paid to athletics. In the normal and elementary schools gymnastic equipment still forms an important adjunct. So far as possible when the weather permits instruction is given out of doors. The students enter into the exercises with great zest and attain a high level of agility under teachers who are specialists. Swimming and skating are now included as part of the course in gymnastics. In the class-room instruction is given in elementary anatomy, the laws of health, rules for first aid to the injured and the part played by gymnastics in the history of the nation. Gymnastics as part of the normal school curriculum is as good an illustration as any of the other branches of the importance which is attached to the teacher in Germany in the promotion of national ideals and national welfare.

In turning to the curriculum of the other states little need be added. Prussia plays such an important part in Germany that her leadership in educational matters is generally accepted. But although the letter of the Prussian curriculum for normal schools is adopted, as for example in the courses for mathematics, drawing and gymnastics, which were adopted in Saxony in 1903, the spirit which animates the work of the class-room is different. While traces of the method which has been described as characteristic of Prussia are still to be found in Saxony, it may be said that generally there is a greater interchange of activity between the instructors and the pupils. In general there is a better adaptation of method to the needs of pupils, who are between the ages of seventeen and twenty, and an absence of that method which is considered appropriate to the elementary schools. The result is seen in more scholarly work, and less of that spirit of submission which is only too apparent in the Prussian normal schools. One point of difference in the curriculum is that Latin is taught in place of French, which, however, has recently been made an alternative. At the end of the course the pupils have a good knowledge of grammar and are able to translate works of ordinary difficulty at sight.

Owing to the fact that the actual normal school course in Bavaria only extends over two years the scope of the subjects is consequently abridged. The same division into fundamental and other subjects is made as in Prussia.

CHAPTER VI

PROFESSIONAL SUBJECTS AND PRACTICE TEACH- ING

The professional subjects, although kept distinct from the academic, are taught concurrently with them throughout the three years of the course. Psychology, principles of education and general method form the subject of the first year's instruction, history of education and principles are taught in the second, and the third year is devoted to administration and general revision. Special method and practice-teaching begin in the second year. Instruction in these subjects is not given by specialists but by the teachers of the academic branches[1] and very frequently by the directors. The method of instruction is much the same as was described in the last chapter. An opportunity of observing the results of this method was afforded in one normal school, where the graduating class was revising immediately before the final examinations. The names of the pupils were written on slips of paper and placed together in one heap, and in another heap were placed a number of questions taken from the professional subjects. Two slips, one from each heap, were then drawn and the pupil whose name was selected had to answer the question which had been drawn. In no case was there any faltering, but the reaction was very much like that of an electric bell to the pressure on the button. While it cannot be denied that the pupils had a knowledge of their subjects, some doubt was left as to its dynamic value.

Psychology is the subject which serves to introduce the pupil to his professional work. Although the advisability of teaching a subject of such difficulty to boys of seventeen may be questioned, it stands logically in its right place to serve as a foundation for the rest of the educational work. As taught at present in Prussia psychology is wholly analytical. Although the regulations recom-

---

[1]Schöppa, pp. 91, 92 and pp. 103-106.

mend a study of child development, very little attention is paid to this branch, and the text-books devote not more than about two pages to it. The observation of children in the practice schools is not made a part of the work. The researches and results of modern psychology receive no mention. In Saxony, however, a new text-book has recently been introduced which embodies the contribution not only of German but also of American psychologists.[2] Elementary logic is included in the study of psychology.

From psychology the transition is made to the selection of subject-matter in the elementary school and general method. This is followed by the theory of education which is carried into the middle of the second year, when the history of education is taken up. The chief emphasis in this subject is laid on the biographical element. After a very brief consideration of education down to the Middle Ages, an intensive study is mode of the development of the elementary school in Germany, with a concentration of attention on the state in which the school is situated. While the educational aspect of the Renaissance and the humanists is treated in brief outline, the effect of the Reformation on the educational development of the country is dealt with at some length. After a detailed account of Luther's work the educational ordinances are discussed. The great educators are treated biographically and stress is laid on a knowledge of dates connected with them. The text-books give selections from the most important educational writings, and the pupils are expected to consult fuller works on the sources. The feature in the instruction of the history of education which can best be approved is the study of the development of the schools in which the future work of the normal school pupils is to be centered. It may be that there is an ulterior motive in placing some emphasis on this part of the work in order to bring into the foreground the part played by the church and the reigning house, but it is undoubtedly an important section of the subject. Here again the regulations are in advance of the practice, for the excellent suggestion that attention should be paid to the relation of educational thought and institutions to the culture of the period is not brought out in the class-room.

The final year of the course is spent in revising psychology, history and principles, and in the study of school administration and

---

[2]Stössner, Pädagogische Psychologie (Leipzig, 1909).

hygiene. In administration the future teacher is made acquainted with the most important regulations in school matters not only of the whole state but of the district in which the normal school is situated. While all the best known principles of school hygiene form part of the instruction in this year, the divorce between practice and precept as regards ventilation, equipment and sanitary arrangements within the normal schools themselves is so great, that the course must leave much to the imagination of the pupils.

Instruction in method begins in the second year, when it is taught indirectly in connection with the model lessons presented by the instructors, and the practice lessons given by the pupils. One period in each week is set aside during the first part of the year in religion, German, and mathematics, and later in other branches for this practice work. Each instructor has charge of the subjects which he teaches in the ordinary course. Before the lesson is presented the instructor discusses the method which will be applied. Several of the pupils are then appointed to write out the lesson-plan and be prepared to present it before a class from the practice-school. The actual lesson may be given either by the instructor, one pupil, or several in turn. Each pupil must have an opportunity of preparing for two lessons in a week. After the lesson, at which the whole class is present, there is a discussion, if that can be called a discussion where the instructor alone carries on the criticism.

In the final year special method is taught for one hour each week in each of the branches of the curriculum. This work is given by the instructors in connection with the academic courses for which they are responsible. In Saxony, however, this practice is not carried out, so that there is a further divorce between subject-matter and method than in Prussia. To this is added, as will be pointed out later, the fact that the critic teacher in the practice-school may be a different person again from either the subject teacher or the instructor in method. The courses deal with the special method of each subject which is taught in the elementary school and the different applications according to the grades. A more significant fact is that the history of the method of each subject forms part of the course. Valuable studies in this field were made under the direction of K. Kehr, himself for a long time the director of a normal school. But the fact that the different methods are not brought to a critical discussion between the instructor and the class detracts somewhat from the value of the study. Frequent opportunities are taken by the teachers to illustrate their lectures by model lessons in the practice-school.

A practice-school is attached to every normal school in the three states which are under discussion. In Prussia[3] these schools vary throughout the state. The regulations prescribe a school with three classes in addition to the ungraded school. While these are the types most commonly found, some schools have five classes, others may be intermediate schools where French is taught, as at Berlin. Each class may contain two grades throughout, or the two highest classes may each contain only one grade. Further the practice-schools are open to both boys and girls. The schools are part of the elementary school system in the districts where they are located, but differ from other schools in being under the direct control of the director of the normal school and so under the authority of the provincial school boards and not of the county authorities. A similar practice holds in Saxony.[4] Such freedom is essential since the normal school faculty must have power to make such arrangements as they regard most beneficial. But while the schools are under the control of the normal schools, the local communities must pay for the upkeep of the schools such expenses as they would have to disburse to maintain a school. The pupils are readily obtained for the graded schools, and in many cases parents prefer to send their children to such schools. The practice as to fees varies; none are charged in Prussia usually, while in Saxony from five to eight marks a month may be charged. Nominally the practice-school should be representative of the best school in the district, and while many are, some suffer from a lack of equipment, which one teacher justified on the ground that it was better for the teachers in practice to have inadequate material as a preparation for the country schools. In Prussia the practice-schools do not have class teachers; the whole of the instruction is given by the student teachers. But in the practice-schools of Saxony there is a critic teacher for each class with the rank of a normal school instructor. The difference between the two systems depends somewhat on the difference in the matter of fees, but more

[3]Bremen, p. 248; Schöppa, p. 77.
[4]Kretzschmar, J. F., p. 88 and p. 142.

perhaps on the difference in the importance attached to the practice work. Under both systems the practice-schools are for administrative purposes and for the arrangement of the students' work under the charge of a member of the normal faculty (*Ordinarius*). No additional salary is paid for what is frequently an additional burden.

The most noteworthy feature in the practice-schools of Prussia is the ungraded school (*Einklassige Schule*), which is usually divided into four sections. This type of school reproduces the conditions of the country and rural schools and is always under the charge of only one student teacher. For these schools there is sometimes a difficulty in obtaining pupils. In some cases they are drawn from children of the very poor by the attraction of free books and presents of clothing once a year. In one school the difficulty was overcome by reserving this class for children from better families, with the result that it was overcrowded. If only the curriculum were adapted for children of rural districts, little could be left to be desired. The subjects of the curriculum, however, only differ from those of the fully graded school in extent but not in character.

There is a difference in the aims which underly the practice work of Prussia on the one hand, and Saxony and Bavaria on the other. While in Prussia the young teacher is generally appointed to the sole charge of a school, in Saxony he is always subordinated to an older teacher, and in Bavaria the major part of the practice is done in the regular schools under the supervision of a district principal at the end of the two years' course in the normal schools. Hence in Prussia the graduate of a normal school must obtain greater facility in practical work than in the other states where the practice partakes more of the character of observation, and is confined to isolated lessons. From four to six hours a week are prescribed by the regulations for practice work for each student in the Prussian normal schools; actually from five to eight hours are found as a rule. Every student is expected during the year of practice to teach religion, German, and arithmetic, and at least one other subject, usually history, and to become familiar with each grade. Generally a good student has opportunities of teaching all the subjects of the curriculum. Each student teaches a subject which is assigned to him for a third or a quarter of a year, the practice varying in different schools. The lessons are prepared under the charge of the instructors of the respective subjects. Lesson notes are written out in full and submitted to the instructor in charge, who makes the necessary alterations and criticisms. All the lesson-plans are drawn up in accordance with the formal steps, either the Herbartian steps or the modifications of Rein or Dörpfeld. The practice teaching is generally satisfactory, although there is a tendency to monotony and sameness of presentation, and a lack of originality or initiative. The students seem to direct their attentions more than necessary to the bright pupils. The supervision of the practice work is in the hands of the instructors according to the subjects which they teach in the normal school. Thus the same instructor is responsible not only for the teaching of the subject-matter, but of method and the students' practice in that subject. In this way unity is maintained. On the other hand the supervision is in danger of being superficial, when the supervisor must look into each of the five to eight rooms of the practice-school during one period. The principle of supervision which is most noticeable is to be sparing in the distribution of praise and, if the situation demands it, to criticise at once without regard to the presence of the class. Not infrequently the supervisors, instead of observing the progress of the student-teacher, take the class into their own hands as soon as they enter the room. The reason which is given for the sharp and immediate criticisms is that, unless they are made on the spot, the supervisors may forget, since no other opportunities for interviews can be provided, as may be seen from the time-table.

In addition to teaching the students also visit and observe each others' practice. The order of observation is usually so arranged that a student visits in the class and subject which he is next to take up himself. When a change of classes and subjects takes place, the students present a lesson in the class which they are about to leave before the whole faculty and the senior class. The theme of the lesson is set by the director.

Once a week the *Ordinarius* holds a class to discuss the work of the practice-school. Two of the students who have observed read very short reports on the practice-teaching, which generally deal with the externalities rather than contain criticisms of real work. The instructor then discusses in a general way the discipline and administration of the school, inquires whether the class diaries are kept up to date, deals with questions of school-room hygiene, the care of the voice, the proper seating of the pupils and any other matters which may have attracted his attention during the past week. In a few minutes he mentions some criticisms made by the other supervisors on the practice-teaching.

It is difficult to characterize the system of practice-teaching in the Prussian normal schools. In so far as the students aim to put into practice not only what they have learned on method in the class-room and strive to carry out a lesson in the same way as they have seen their instructors teach, the system may be called apprenticeship training.[5] On the other hand since the supervisors have so little time to spend in the class-rooms of the practice-school, there is an element of the laboratory system, if the students were only encouraged to use their own resources and initiative. But while not expected to be finished teachers on leaving the normal schools, the students are supposed to be sufficiently advanced to take the sole charge of an ungraded school.

Saxony and Bavaria offer a contrast to the Prussian system. The fact that the unity between theory and practice is maintained with some difficulty in Saxony has already been mentioned. But less time is also given to practice-teaching. This may be due to the fact that the pupils in the practice-school pay fees, and that the graduating students are not appointed to independent positions, so that their training under supervision practically continues for several years after leaving the normal school. Very little importance is attached in the leaving examination to the practice-lesson. Introduction into the work of the practice-school begins in the first year of the normal school proper, when the students observe model lessons. In the last two years four hours a week are devoted to practice work or observation in the school. The subjects of instruction are not assigned for any length of time as in Prussia, but several students may prepare to teach during part of a period. The classes are divided into groups of six and assigned to the charge of the critic teachers, who are always present. The model lessons are followed by a brief statement from the critic teacher of the essential points of the lesson, the lessons of the students are subjected to the criticisms of the teacher at the conclusion of the lesson. There is no interruption on the part of the

---

[5]See Dewey, The Relation of Theory and Practice in the Education of Teachers.

critic-teacher during the presentation of a lesson by a student. Thus the Saxon system differs from the Prussian in being extensive, with an emphasis on observation of good teaching rather than practice.

The energy of the students and instructors in the last few months of the final year is devoted to preparation for the leaving examination, (*Entlassungsprüfung*), which also serves as the first teachers examination. The examination is conducted with all formality by a board consisting of the members of the faculty, a commissioner who represents the provincial school board, and a representative of the county authority in which the school is located. The denominations are allowed to send representatives to the examination in religion, and they have the power to refuse to pass a candidate who is deficient in this subject. Candidates for the teaching profession who have not been trained in a normal school may be examined at the same time, but such cases are very rare. All candidates must present the written work of the year preceding the examination. As is the case with all examinations, there is a division into oral and written parts. The written examination consists of the following subjects: (1) An essay on a subject from pedagogy or German literature. (2) and (3) Short essays on religious and historical topics. (4) Translation from a foreign language. (5) The composition of a choral piece of music by those who take the examination in organ-playing and harmony. (6) Written notes for a lesson set by the examiners within a subject selected by the candidates themselves.[6]

In the oral examination candidates are tested in pedagogy, method, religion, German, history, and a foreign language. Those candidates who were conditioned at the end of their second year in mathematics, natural science and geography may now be examined in these subjects. All candidates must present a lesson in the presence of the examiners. Deficiency in one subject may be annulled by good work in others, but a satisfactory standard must be reached in pedagogy, religion, German and history. On the other hand candidates who have shown particular brilliance in the written work may be excused from the oral examination. Four grades are given on the examination, "very good," "good," "satisfactory," and "unsatisfactory." The successful candidates receive

---

[6] Schöppa, pp. 139-147.

certificates bearing their names and some personal facts, the nature of their training, reports on their industry and conduct, the decisions on their written work, and the marks which they received in the individual subjects and on the lesson. If a candidate presents himself for the examination in organ-playing, the certificate contains some report on his ability.

The leaving examination in the Saxon[7] normal schools is similar to that in Prussia. In the written test questions are set in history, geography, and natural science, as well as arithmetic and geometry, a translation from Latin into German, and the plan for a catechism. In the practical examination candidates are tested in writing, drawing and gymnastics, and two lessons, one of which must be in religion, must be presented.

In Bavaria the final examination at the end of the two years' course covers all the subjects of the curriculum. The successful candidates are admitted to begin their practical training.

In all cases success in the leaving examinations entitles the candidates to the privilege of serving in the army for one year as volunteers. This privilege together with the nature of the first appointment held by the elementary school teachers in the different states will be treated in the following chapter.

---

[7]Kretzschmar, J. F., p. 552.

CHAPTER VII

THE TEACHER AT WORK

In dealing with the German teacher two essential features stand out prominently. No one can serve in a public school who has not passed through a period of training, and no teacher is definitely appointed until he has served a period of probation of at least two years. Thus few teachers receive their permanent appointment until they are over twenty-two years of age. That the candidates for the elementary school positions are at the disposal of the state authorities for periods varying from three years in Saxony to five years in Prussia in return for the free tuition, which they had received in the normal schools, has already been referred to as one of the conditions of entry. The importance of this fact becomes clear, when it is mentioned that three years ago the Prussian government availed itself of this right to draft teachers from all parts of the state to the Polish province, and when the supply of teachers was a pressing problem at the same period, teachers were moved about as need arose.

The first appointment which the candidate, on leaving the normal school, receives is temporary. The appointing authority in Prussia is the Department for Ecclesiastical and School Affairs of the Royal County.[1] The practice varies, however. In the eastern parts of Prussia the teacher may be selected by the town councils and those patrons who have seignorial rights over schools from the list of qualified candidates. Where the school patron does not exercise the right of appointing the teacher, the county authority steps in, and the right may also be voluntarily surrendered. In the western provinces of the state the general practice is for the county authority to make the appointment.

In Saxony the first appointment of teachers is made by the District Inspection Board, (*Bezirksschulinspektion*)[2] and in Bavaria

---

[1]Bremen, p. 363; Handbuch für Lehrer und Lehrerinnen, pp. 6-8.
[2]Seydewitz, pp. 69 and 124.

by the District Administrative Board (*Kreisregierung*).[3] In both of these states the teacher who only holds a provisional appointment bears the title of assistant teacher (*Hilfslehrer*).

In all cases the appointment of a probationer is terminable on notice, the only instance where this practice holds in the German teachers' profession. The salaries of teachers during this period will be given below with those of permanently appointed teachers.

The first appointment in Prussia is in all cases held in an ungraded rural school, where the probationer is the only teacher. In this practice lies the strength of the Prussian training system, for the probationary period must be regarded as a continuation of the training. Here for the first time the young teacher is left to his own resources in the exercise of a position independent of all assistance but that of the local and district inspector. The qualification of the local inspector, usually the pastor, has already been dealt with.[4] As will be shown later the district inspector appears so rarely that it may be said that in his first appointment the elementary school teacher must face all the problems of school management in the best way that he can. Very frequently the school is situated in a community in which the teacher cannot find congenial society. If the pastor is sympathetic and not inclined to claim a traditional superiority, the teacher's lot need not be one of difficulty. That the majority do not abuse their first taste of independence or submit to its temptations is due rather to the traditions of the profession than to the training of the normal school. And there are many teachers who, once they have overcome the initial difficulties, prefer to remain in charge of an ungraded, rural school rather than to seek promotion in a town. In the country they can, if successful, win a position in the community next in influence to the pastor. Local school traditions can be established and a friendship maintained with the parents on a basis of common interests. The rural teacher obtains an acquaintance with local conditions which can contribute to a solution of many of the problems which beset him. In such cases, and they appear to be frequent, the teaching profession truly becomes a calling inspired by devotion to high ideals. It is largely through a recognition of this that the government withholds permission to the elementary school teacher to

[3] Englmann, p. 180.
[4] Ch. II.

proceed to the University. There is a fear that the university trained teacher will be unwilling to take up the duties of a rural school. On the other side it is argued[5] with truth that so long as men with university training will be found to take up pastoral duties and the practice of medicine in a remote village, so long will there be found men to take charge of the schools there, provided of course that the services are adequately recognized financially. And until recently the salaries have not been such as to keep capable teachers in the country. Nor has care been taken to make other conditions attractive. Frequently the school-house is in a poor state. Although a house is provided for the teacher, no steps are taken to insist that it is kept in a sanitary condition.

Legally the teacher of an ungraded school may have under his charge at one time eighty children. If this number is exceeded or the school-room is not large enough, the pupils may be divided into two sections, each attending one half day. Where the number of pupils exceeds a hundred, a decree recommends the employment of a second teacher. It is significant that the Kaiser has said that to teach a class of seventy children is "nothing but human torture." But as recently as 1908[6] cases could be quoted where single teachers had charge of from 90 to 200 pupils. With the increase in salary, there will come an increase in the supply of teachers and a more equable distribution of the pupils. In consequence of these conditions the curriculum of the ungraded school is limited to essentials. Religion, German, arithmetic, drawing, singing and gymnastics together with a subject which goes under the name of object lessons (*Realien*) are taught. It will be recognized that the problem of the rural school is not faced.

The ungraded schools are divided into three sections, lower, middle, and upper. With the exception of the lower section which receives twenty hours instruction, the rest of the school has thirty hours per week. In addition to the work of the school and such church duties as are allotted to him, the teacher during his first appointment must find time to prepare for the second examination for permanent appointment. In view of the lack of train-

---

[5] *Padagogisches Jahrbuch*, 1905, p. 177.

[6] See the speech of Herr Tews on *Lehrermangel* in Bericht über die deutsche Lehrerversammlung in Dortmund, 1908.

ing in independent judgment this is no easy task for the young teacher. The result is that short-cut methods of preparation are chosen and any of the numerous cram-books which are edited for the purpose are used. In practical work, however, the problems of the ungraded class-room offer good opportunities for making progress. The means for the further training of teachers will be treated in the next chapter.

In Saxony and Bavaria the candidates for positions in elementary schools serve the period of probation in a graded school, but have charge of a class. *The Instructions for the Operation of the Elementary School Law* (August 25, 1874)[7] in Saxony expressly prescribe the appointment of assistant teachers (*Hilfslehrer*) in schools where they can avail themselves of the advice and guidance of older teachers. Usually not more than one assistant teacher may be appointed to six regular teachers.[8] In Bavaria there are similar regulations recommending the assistant teachers to the care and supervision of the older teachers.[9]

The qualification for permanent appointment in an elementary school depends on success in the second examination.[10] which candidates must take within a period of two to five years after leaving the normal school. The period here mentioned is that which is allowed in Prussia. Permission to present for the examination depends on the report of the inspector of the district in which the candidate has been employed. Where permission is refused, the reasons are given. By this means there is a method of eliminating the unfit or the undesirable before the examination is reached. The examining commissions are constituted in the same way as those which conduct the first examinations, and the examination takes place at the normal schools. So far as possible candidates are assigned to the normal schools where they received their training. Candidates who are not assigned to their own normal schools feel that an additional difficulty has been introduced into the examination. Their first aim is to obtain as much information as they can about the instructors, more particularly their weak points. There is no doubt that familiarity with the surroundings and an acquaintance with

---

[7]Seydewitz, p. 196.
[8]Ibid., p. 229.
[9]Englmann, p. 180.
[10]Bremen, pp. 282-285.

the idiosyncrasies of the examiners removes some of the terrors of the examination. And from the other side the examiner's knowledge of the candidates in some cases means the difference between a pass and failure. In many cases allowance is made for poor work due to nervousness or other causes because of previous acquaintance with the candidate while in the normal school. The examination is in no sense a revision of the work of the normal school, but a test of the efficiency and the development of the candidate in professional power since his first appointment. In applying for permission to be admitted to the examination candidates must give evidence of the professional writings which they have read and of the study of some special subject. Particular stress is laid in the examination on progress in theory, method and practice of education. The examination consists of two parts, written and oral. In the written part an essay on some topic from the field of pedagogy is to be done in four hours. Neither the quality nor quantity of these essays is usually of a high standard. Rarely are more than one or two sheets of foolscap handed in at the end of the period, and even in this short space the tendency to talk around the point is not avoided. On the other hand the examiners set a high standard and rarely does a candidate obtain the first mark. One excellent essay was recently marked down because the candidate had ventured to criticize a ministerial regulation. As a general rule opportunity is taken to drag in irrelevant matter which smacks of the cram-book. The oral examination includes questions on the theory and practice of education, a knowledge of the psychological basis of method, the history of education and the contribution of prominent pedagogues and particularly the history of the Prussian elementary school. An acquaintance with the administrative work of a school and with government regulations on education is demanded. Questions may be asked on the method of at least two of the fundamental subjects, German, religion, history and mathematics. Further, candidates are examined on the subject of which they have made a special study and which may be selected from any of the academic subjects of the normal schools. The scope of the examination is completed by the presentation of a lesson in the practice school. The subject is assigned at a day's notice, but the wishes of the candidates are considered in the matter of the branch of the curriculum and the grade which is to be taught. Here again the candidates expend some effort in discovering details about the pupils in the practice schools and the location of the brighter pupils. A lesson-plan fully elaborated must be handed in before the lesson is given. The plans show a painfully exaggerated effort to work out every lesson, no matter what the nature of the subject may be, in conformity with the five Herbartian steps. This is all the more remarkable because this system has generally been discarded. The consequence generally, in the cases which were observed, was a difficulty in handling the lesson where the pupils did not respond in the expected manner. Allowing for the nervousness of the candidates, which was in no degree lessened by the outspoken criticisms and the interruptions of the examiners, the lessons did not reach a good standard. The number of candidates did not admit of sufficient time to complete any one lesson. There appeared to be considerable unfairness in the test. The formality, the strange pupils, the objections of the examiners to which the candidates were not allowed to reply and which the pupils took in with open ears to the extent of being able to infer what grade a candidate was likely to get, all contributed to the impression that none but the strongest and most self-possessed of the candidates could do themselves justice. And this fact was amply confirmed by a comparison between the grades given by the examiners and the reports of the district inspectors. In some cases the candidates were allotted subjects or sections of subjects which they had no opportunity of teaching in an ungraded school. A candidate who obtained a failing mark might receive permission to present another lesson, if the quality of his work in the rest of the examination justified such a course. It is in such cases that the previous acquaintance of the examiners with the candidates is found to be useful. On the whole, however, the retention of this part of the examination cannot be justified. It would be far more just to the candidates, and more reasonable in practice to rely on the judgment of the inspectors, provided that they were in a position to pay more frequent visits to the individual teachers than they do at present. The injustice of such a test as at present constituted is further emphasized by the fact that its result is critical for the future career of the teacher, for on the grade which he now obtains depend his chances of promotion into a town system with a good salary scale, as well as of entering one of the special courses in Berlin.

A certificate is granted on the general result of the examination. In the case of unsatisfactory work in the lesson, or pedagogy, or two of the fundamental subjects, the certificate may be refused. Otherwise credit is given for good subjects to counterbalance unsatisfactory results in others. The possession of the certicate carries with it the qualification for permanent appointment, which, however, cannot be confirmed until the candidates have passed through the period of military service.

Similar provisions are found in the other states. In Saxony the Eligibility Examination (*Wahlfähigkeitsprüfung*)[11] must be taken three years after leaving the normal schools and in case of failure can only be twice repeated. With the exception of the omission of the examination in French and the addition of the preparation of a catechetical lesson-plan the regulations are so much like those of Prussia that they need no further comment. On the result of the examination depends not only the right to a permanent appointment, but also permission to proceed to the University of Leipzig, which is given outright to those candidates who receive the first mark, "excellent," in the examination, and by special consent of the Minister to those candidates who receive the mark "quite good" (Ib).

The Appointment Examination (*A stellungsprüfung*)[12] in Bavaria differs from the above only in extent and scope, for the written examination includes in addition to the essay papers in educational theory, geography, history, arithmetic, mathematics, religion, natural science, drawing and harmony. The title and the first ten lines of the essay serve as a test in caligraphy, while the essay and the papers on educational theory are also examined for spelling. The oral examination includes religion, German, school administration and music. There is also a test in gymnastics. No provision is made for an examination in practical teaching. Candidates, however, are only admitted to the examination if the district school authorities report that their practical work and religious life are satisfactory, and if they are "politically blameless." Candidates who fail to pass the examina-

---

[11]Kretzschmar, J. F., pp. 560-569.
[12]Englmann, pp. 194-196.

tion in three attempts are excluded from the teaching profession.

At some period after leaving the normal school and before he can be confirmed in a permanent appointment, every German teacher must satisfy the authorities that he has performed his military duties. By an order of the Cabinet which came into force in 1900 teachers in elementary schools, who have passed the leaving examination of a normal school, receive the privilege of serving only for one year. This year may be spent either at the expense of the state or at personal expense. In the former case (*Einjährige aktive Militärdienst*) the soldier is subjected to the ordinary discipline of the service; in the latter he purchases his own equipment, does not live in barracks, has some power of selecting his regiment, and is not subjected to the menial duties of military life in barracks. An active campaign is being carried on by teachers' associations to bring the advantages of the one-year service as a volunteer to the general notice of teachers, and more particularly to advise them of the cost of this course and to inform parents how they may prepare by insurance of a boy as soon as he enters on the period of training in order to meet the expenses. The cost of such a year's service is on an average 1400 M. ($350).[13] Teachers in permanent service can claim their salaries during the year of military service.[14] In 1906-1907 of the elementary school teachers in military service 40.26 per cent. were serving as one-year volunteers.[15] The leaders among the elementary school teachers attach importance to an increase of those in their ranks who avail themselves of this privilege, which carries a certain amount of social prestige with it.

Candidates for positions in elementary schools are officially recommended to perform the year of service as soon as possible after leaving the normal schools.[16] A more usual practice seems to be to enter on the military duties after passing the second examination, in order on the one hand to have an unbroken period of preparation for the examination and to save towards the expenses of the year of service, and on the other to enter on an ap-

---

[13]Handbuch für Lehrer und Lehrerinnen, p. 90.
[14]Ibid., p. 13.
[15]*Pädagogisches Jahrbuch*, 1907, p. 177.
[16]Bremen, p. 388.

pointment without the necessity of later taking leave of absence for a year. The period of military service is regarded as an interruption of the professional career. But upon it as much as upon the passing of the second examination depends the permanent and definite appointment of a teacher in a German elementary school.[17]

The appointment of teachers in Prussia is made by the local authorities from the list of eligible candidates.[18] In school communities with twenty-five teachers or less the selection is made from a list of three candidates suggested by the county department. In towns the selection is made by the town authorities on the recommendation of the school committee. Where a school is under seignorial patronage, the patron has the right to select the candidate in consultation with the local school committee. In every case, however, the confirmation of the selection is made by the county department, which through its officials gives the record of the appointment to the teacher on his introduction to his position.[19]

Candidates for vacant school positions are obtained by advertising the vacancies, but in the cases of the better school systems there is no dearth of applicants. The vacancies are announced in the current or professional newspapers, or in the journals which make a special feature of this form of advertisement. Information about the candidates may be obtained by correspondence, by inviting the candidate to appear and present a lesson before a committee, or by visiting the candidates in the schools where they are located at the time.[20] The last practice as involving the least amount of inconvenience is recommended officially. In such a case the superintendent or other professional officer of the school system is sent to visit the candidates. Where the candidate is invited to appear and present a lesson, only the professional or semi-professional members of the school committee are permitted to attend. The town councillors are not permitted to take any part whatever. In the case of the rural schools, the

---

[17]Plüschke, Die städtischen Schuldeputationen und ihr Geschäftskreis, p. 204.
[18]Ibid., pp. 672-674.
[19]Ibid., pp. 672–674 and pp. 718-720.
[20]Ibid., pp. 174-176.

model lesson is largely employed as a means of making the acquaintance of the candidates rather than as a professional test.

On the power of selecting candidates only two restrictions[21] are placed by the higher authorities. It is not considered advisable to encourage a young teacher to change his positions too frequently, and the county authority has the power to refuse to confirm an appointment in such a case. Teachers must be encouraged to stay in one place as long as possible in order to benefit to the full extent by the experience. It is felt that the practice of allowing teachers to change frequently might involve the danger of withdrawing teachers from the rural schools. To the same cause is due the restriction that young teachers should not be appointed to positions in town schools systems. In this way the interests of the country schools and the systems with low salary scales are safeguarded. The denominational character of the position is, of course, to be taken into consideration.

On receiving his appointment the teacher is ceremoniously introduced to the school and his colleagues either by the district or the local school inspector. Considerable importance is attached to the ceremony of introduction. In no case will its omission be disregarded. It is incompatible with the position of the teacher and the significance of his official position in the school and the community to omit the ceremony.[22] At the same time he receives the record of his appointment (*Ernennungsurkunde* or *Vokation*). This certificate of appointment may by law include or exclude[23] certain conditions. For example higher qualifications than those established by law cannot be demanded. No teacher can renounce his right to a pension. Appointment for a definite time or upon notice cannot be made. Contributions towards pensions or widows' funds cannot be exacted. No teacher can be compelled to give instruction in a continuation school without remuneration. But the certificate may include a condition to the effect that a teacher must in case of need do substitute work and give additional religious instruction where necessary. The appointment is made to a school or a school system and not to a grade or to teach a group of subjects.

---

[21]Ibid., p. 177.
[22]Ibid., p. 180.
[23]Ibid., p. 187.

Once appointed the teacher cannot be dismissed except for grave breach of discipline or gross neglect of duties. In any case the only authority competent to deal with the teachers are the state officials, the local and district inspectors.[24] The local school authorities have no direct power over the teacher whatever. The inspectors have the power to warn and censure and to inflict a fine up to 9 M. The teacher is a servant of the state and local interference would be regarded as an interference with the rights of the state. If the teacher desires leave of absence, he is referred to the state officials, the inspectors, the county departments, or the Oberpräsident according to the length of the period of absence which is desired. If the teacher has any complaints or any appeals to make, he does so to the same authorities. To these he is also responsible for keeping the official documents, the class register, the reports on the scholars, a record of the work done, and a list of the punishments inflicted. There is thus the apparent anomaly of a local authority maintaining schools and paying, very often, the larger part of the teachers' salaries without power of control over the teaching body. In large towns the superintendent is also the district school inspector. In smaller areas matters of difficulty can be referred by the local body to those who have competent authority.

In Saxony[25] and Bavaria[26] the same principle of selection of candidates by one body and confirmation of the appointment by another is found. In Saxony all vacancies must be reported to the District Board of Inspection, which advertises them; in Bavaria the appointing authority is the *Kreisregierung,* which must have the support of the church authorities where church services are attached to the school position. The model lesson in Saxony is presented before the district or local inspector or the school principal, and the power of selection is vested in the local school authority with the cooperation of the pastor. In Bavaria the practice of demanding the presentation of a lesson does not appear to prevail. The selecting bodies may be either local communities, corporations, pastors, or private patrons. For appointments in towns candidates must have obtained either the first or second mark in the appointments examination, and the first

---

[24]Ibid., pp. 195-196.
[25]Seydewitz, pp. 199-204.
[26]Englmann, pp. 205, 224, 226.

mark for conduct. A curious feature in connection with appointments in Bavaria is the levy of a tax of 10 per cent. on the value of the salary or, in the case of promotion, on the value of the increase in salary. In the oath of office, which is also administered in Prussia and Saxony, in addition to the promise of loyalty and proper performance of duties, teachers must undertake not to join secret societies.[27] The ceremonious introduction into office, which is found in Saxony,[28] is not mentioned in the Bavarian regulations. As in Prussia the teachers in the other states are subject to the disciplinary measures only of the state authorities, except that in Bavaria the local school authority may warn and censure.[29]

The principle which underlies the salary systems in Germany is very simple. The states in each case fix a legal minimum scale, which must be paid to all teachers, and the first care of the central authorities is to assist in the maintenance of this standard by contributing to the funds of local bodies for this purpose. In the poor rural communities the whole salary of a teacher is often paid in this way. For larger systems the state subsidy forms only a very small fraction of the salary schedule. The minimum scale established over a large area has the disadvantage that in some parts it may be rigidly adhered to without being commensurate with the cost of living there. It must always be remembered, however, that in addition to salary the German teacher also receives a house or compensation for rent, proportionate to the local rates, and that he can look forward to a pension on his retirement, and provision for his family on his death. Comparing relative values and differences in purchasing power of money, the elementary school teacher receives a higher remuneration for his services than his colleagues in England, France or America.

After an agitation for a revision of the scale of salaries the Prussian teachers have succeeded in procuring the passage of a salary law which came into effect last year (*Das Lehrerbesoldungsgesetz vom 26 Mai, 1909*).[30] The great variety and dis-

---

[27]Englmann, p. 226.

[28]Seydewitz, p. 203.

[29]Englmann, p. 266.

[30]Glattfelter, Das Lehrerbesoldungsgesetz vom 26 Mai, 1909 (Düsseldorf, 1909), It should be pointed out that the first paragraph of the *Rep. of the Com. of Ed.* on the question (1909, p. 452), is not correct.

parity in the salary scales in different parts of the state, the rapid increase of prices for the commodities of life, and the dearth of teachers were some of the compelling factors in changing the law.

In place of the minimum salary of 900 M. ($225) established by the previous salary law of 1897, the new law fixes the minimum at 1400 M. ($350) per year. The scale rises to the maximum by nine increments. The first increment accrues after seven years' service and the others in periods of three years thereafter. The first two increments amount each to 200 M. ($50), the next two are of the value of 250 M. ($62.50) each, followed by five of 200 M. Thus the maximum after thirty years service is 3300 M. ($825). A new feature of the law is that the sums paid as compensation for rent no longer depend on local circumstances, but are fixed once and for all according to the class of city to which the school is situated. The compensation amounts to 800 M. ($200) in cities of the first class; 650 M. ($162.50) in cities of the second class; 540 M. ($135) in cities of the third class; 450 M. ($102.50) in cities of the fourth class; and 330 M. ($82.50) in cities of the fifth class. Further for purposes of the pension the rent-indemnity is included in the calculation of the salary. In the salaries of teachers holding a provisional appointment only, and of those not over four years in service the minimum mentioned above may be curtailed by one-fifth.

In Saxony the present salary law[31] was passed in 1908 and came into force at the beginning of last year. Assistant teachers by that law receive a commencing salary of 900 M. ($225). This was increased in the second year to 1000 M. ($250), and 1100 M. ($275) in the third year. Teachers holding a definite appointment have a commencing salary of 1500 M. ($375) per year rising by six triennial increments of 200 M. ($50) to 2700 M. ($675) and thence by two triennial increments of 150 M. ($37.50) to 3000 M. ($750). As distinguished from the Prussian system the expense of the increments is borne entirely by the state in Saxony since 1900. To the salary must also be added a

[31]Pätzold, Geschichte des Volksschulwesens im Königreich Sachsen, p. 194 (Leipzig, 1908).

house or compensation for rent, which is included with the salary in calculating the amount of the pensions.[32]

In Bavaria[33] assistant teachers receive a salary of 820 M. ($205) per year until definitely appointed, when a minimum of 1200 M. ($300) is paid. The increments in salary begin after five years' service. The first five increments, paid at varying intervals of five, three, two and five years, amount to 90 M. ($22.50) each, and are followed by four increments of 120 M. ($30) paid at intervals of five years. Thus at the end of forty years' service a teacher would be in receipt of 930 M. plus 1200 M. ($532.50), provided that he started at the legal minimum, which is not at all probable. As in Prussia and Saxony a house or compensation for rent is provided.

The following table[34] will give a comparative view of the salaries which are paid in the three states:

YEAR OF LIFE	SALARY		
	Prussia	Saxony	Bavaria
Twenty-fifth....................	$333.20	$357.00	$321.30
Fortieth.......................	595.00	595.00	499.80
Forty-ninth....................	737.80	714.00	618.80
Fifty-first.....................	785.50	714.00	618.80
Fifty-second...................	785.50	714.00	666.40

To the present value of these salaries must be added the expectation in each case of a pension, as well as of provision for widows and orphans. In Prussia[35] a teacher, if incapacitated for further work, may retire on a pension after ten years' service which amounts to 20/60ths of the salary at the time of retirement. After the tenth year of service 1/60th is added annually to this sum. In no case can a pension amount to more than 45/60ths of a teacher's total income, but this sum accrues at the age of 65. Towards the payment of pensions the state contributes 700 M. ($175). All school authorities responsible for bringing the pen-

---

[32]Seydewitz, pp. 73, 206.

[33]Englmann, pp. 272 311.

[34]*Rept. U. S. Com. Educ.*, 1909, p. 453.

[35]Glattfelter, Das Lehrererbesoldungsgesetz vom 26 Mai, 1909, etc. pp. 103-121.

sions up to the statutory limit must deposit the requisite fund with the county authority, which undertakes the charge of managing and distributing the fund at a small cost.

Not only is provision made for pensioning teachers on their retirement from service, but since 1899 the state by law grants support to the widows and orphans of deceased teachers.[36]   A widow is entitled to 40 per cent. of the pension to which her husband was or would have been entitled at the time of his death. Such a sum, since 1907, must not be less than 300 M. ($75) nor more than 3500 M. ($875) per year. Children, if the mother is still alive, are entitled each to one-fifth of the sum paid to the mother; otherwise each to one-third of what their mother would have received.   In no case, however, may the combined sum of the receipts of the widow and orphans be equal to the amount of the pension to which the deceased was entitled.   The claim to this provision ceases on marriage of the widow or with the attainment of the eighteenth birthday by the orphans.   Towards the widows and orphans fund the state contributes 420 M. ($105) for each widow, and 84 M. ($21) or 140 M. ($35) for each orphan, the sum depending on whether the mother is alive or not. The first payment of claims is made three months after the death of the teacher, but during this period the full amount of the deceased's pension is paid to his family (*Gnadenquartal*).   As in the case of the pension all school authorities responsible for the payment of support to widows and orphans must deposit the requisite sums with the county treasury.

In Saxony[37] the state bears the whole cost of pensions, except in those cases where local authorities have made provision for the payment of pensions equal to the legal minimum.   The scale is somewhat more liberal than in Prussia.   The pension may under satisfactory circumstances be claimed after ten years of service, counting only those served after the twenty-fifth year. The amount which may then be paid is thirty per cent. of the salary at the time of retirement.   From this sum the scale rises gradually up to eighty per cent. of the salary at the end of forty years of service or the attainment of the sixty-fifth birthday. For the widows and orphans of deceased teachers there is a pro-

---

[36]Glattfelter, pp. 137-149.
[37]Kretzschmar, J. F., pp. 603-611.

vision for each of one-fifth of the salary last drawn. In the case of full orphans three-tenths of this sum is paid until the child reaches the age of eighteen.[38]

For Bavaria[39] it is difficult to make anything more than a general statement on the pension system, since unlike the other states no legal standard prevails. District pension bureaus (*Kreispensionsanstalt*) exist to which all teachers must contribute. An entrance fee of 24 M. ($6) is exacted, and an annual subscription of from one to two per cent. of the pension to which the contributor would be entitled if he retired at the time of payment. The state contributes 600 M. ($150) towards the pension of a teacher who retires before completing forty years of service, and 640 M. ($160) per year where forty years of service have been completed. But the pensions are only paid to teachers so long as they are incapacitated from active service. If they recover and take a new appointment, they must again resume their contributions to the pension fund. The scales vary very largely throughout the state but a minimum of 900 M. ($225) has been established for teachers permanently appointed. In addition to the district pension bureaus many of the towns have their own departments for this purpose, to which the teachers must contribute. In the same way all teachers are compelled since 1902 to be members of a society which has for its object the support of the widows and orphans of teachers.[40] The entrance fees and annual contributions vary widely, with the consequence that the amount of the payments to the widows and orphans shows an equal variation. The state, however, assures to each widow the annual sum of 300 M. ($75), to each full orphan 150 M. ($37.50), and to each orphan whose mother is still living 100 M. ($25) per year up to 16, if a girl, up to 18, if a boy. The state contributions are additional to the sums which may be paid locally. The towns have their own systems of insurance for these purposes and different scales of payments.

In order to afford a basis of comparison for the values of the salaries the following table, selected from two hundred returns

---

[38]Ibid., pp. 616-618.

[39]Englmann, pp. 352-395.

[40]Ibid., pp. 395-436.

by the Saxon Teachers' Association, is given. The table represents the expenditure of five teachers:[41]

EXPENDITURE ON:	YOUNG UNMARRIED TEACHER	CHILDLESS FAMILY Husband 20	FAMILY WITH 1–2 CHILDREN Husband 30	3–4 CHILDREN Husband 40	CHILDREN GROWN UP Husband 50
Food..................	540M	840M	960M	1200M	1200M
Clothing and laundry...	250	300	500	600	700
Fire and ighting.......	60	100	100	100	100
Taxes and savings......	100	150	200	200	200
Supplies...............	60	100	100	100	100
Help..................	60	80	80	80	100
Health and physical welfare...............	150	160	160	200	200
Schooling.............	......	......	......	200	600
Educational...........	100	50	50	50	50
Extras................	280	220	250	270	350
	1600	2000	2400	3000	3600

These lived rent free.

[41]*Pädagogisches Jahrbuch*, 1907, p. 182.

CHAPTER VIII

THE TRAINING OF TEACHERS IN SERVICE

However perfect a system of training teachers previous to their entry into service may be, it must be recognized that the utmost that a normal school can be expected to do is not to produce finished teachers but to fill the pupils with a strong professional feeling and to inspire them with a desire to continue their further education. But in addition to professional spirit and personal ambition, other stimuli must be provided and some organization must be established to assist the teachers in their further training. In the following chapter the means which are adopted in the three states, for the training of teachers in service will be dealt with. A distinction must, however, be made in the provisions for further training according as they are formal, established by and under the supervision of the state, and informal, including such organizations as partake of a private character.

The principle that teachers at the beginning of their careers require more training than that which is given in the normal schools has been fully recognized in Germany. It is upon this principle that permanent appointment in an elementary school follows only after a period of probation, extending from two to five years. The examinations for permanent appointment have already been dealt with in the preceding chapter. In Prussia there are in addition promotional examinations for appointments in intermediate schools (*Mittelschulen*) and higher girls' schools and as principals of elementary schools. As was pointed out in an earlier chapter these two examinations must also be passed in order to qualify for appointment in a normal school.

The examination for teachers in intermediate schools is open to elementary school teachers who have already passed the second examination, ministers, candidates for positions in secondary schools and candidates in theology. The examination, which is

97

both written and oral, consists of pedagogy and two subjects selected from the following and, so far as possible, related to each other: Religion, German, French, English, history, geography, mathematics, botany and zoology, physics and chemistry with mineralogy. A dissertation, for the preparation of which eight weeks are allowed, and the presentation of a lesson before the examiners complete the examination.[1]

To qualify for the position of principal of an elementary school with six or more classes or for any of the higher positions, with the exception of appointments in secondary schools, candidates must have passed the principals' examination, which may be taken three years after the examination for appointment in intermediate schools. The subjects of the examination are mainly concerned with the theory and practice of education and school management. The thesis, for which eight weeks are allowed, is on some phase of these studies. In the oral examination questions are taken from the general field of pedagogy, special method, school administration and state regulations, the chief types of school apparatus and aids for instruction, and popular and child literature. Where it is sought to obtain qualifications for a principalship in a school where a foreign language is taught, there is a further test in this language.[2]

Promotional examinations of these kinds are not found in Saxony or Bavaria. In the former state there is, however, a provision that only those who obtained not less than the second mark in the eligibility examination may be appointed as principals of schools.[3] Whether the Prussian system of promoting by examinations is to be recommended is at least an open question, although the examination system is considered to be one of the elements of strength in the teaching profession of that state. The qualities which are required in a school principal are not of a type which can be submitted to measurement by examination.

The systems of inspection in the three states were mentioned in the second chapter. It was there pointed out that with the exception of Saxony the inspectors are preponderatingly from the clerical order. Not only is it the case that the majority of the

---

[1]Schöppa, p. 153.
[2]Ibid., p. 163.
[3]Seydewitz, p. 195.

inspectors are not professional teachers, but their number is at present inadequate to perform to any extent the function of training teachers in service. Usually a district inspector (*Kreis-schulinspektor*) in Prussia[4] has two hundred teachers under him. They are expected to visit every school once a year, but frequently not more than one inspection in two years can be made. In Saxony[5] only one visit in two years is expected from the district inspector (*Bezirksschulinspektor*), while in Bavaria[6] the district inspector is expected to pay one visit each year to the schools of his district. In every case the local inspector has opportunities to visit the schools more frequently, but such visits are rather elements of irritation than of service to the teachers.

Of a more formal character in the systems of training of teachers in service are the conferences. The most important in Prussia[7] and Saxony[8] are conducted once a year by the district inspectors, which all teachers in elementary schools are obliged to attend. In Prussia a small remuneration is paid since 1897 to cover the necessary expenses incurred in coming to the meeting. The conferences are under the presidency of the inspectors, and usually include a lecture on a subject which has previously been assigned to one of the teachers of the district, dealing with some question of pedagogy or general method or other topic of current interest; a model lesson or a lecture on special method may also form the subject for such meetings. In each case a discussion follows. Recently the practice has grown up in Prussia of inviting the district medical officers to teachers' conferences to address the teachers on school hygiene, dietetics, alcoholism or tuberculosis. In addition to the general annual conferences the inspectors at their discretion may hold more frequent meetings of the assistant teachers, and special conferences with school principals.

Bavaria, however, has a more comprehensive system for the training of teachers during the early years of their service. In each district a school principal of some ability is appointed by the District Administrative Board (*Kreisregierung*) to hold an ex-

---

[4]Kretzschmar, Fr., p. 59.
[5]Seydewitz, p. 227.
[6]Englmann, p. 73.
[7]Plüschke, pp. 598-607; Kretzschmar, Fr., p. 60; Bremen, p. 575.
[8]Seydewitz, pp. 118 and 229.

tension course for the purpose of continuing the education and inspiring young teachers with the seriousness of their calling and a strong professional spirit. All teachers not holding a permanent appointment, those teachers who obtained only the third or lowest qualifying mark in the appointment examination, and teachers who are not performing satisfactory service are obliged to attend these extension courses.[9] Other teachers may attend voluntarily provided that there is no conflict with their other duties. Programmes and text-books are suggested annually for private study. Libraries have been instituted in each district under the charge of the directing principal and a committee of teachers. The books which are useful for such libraries are suggested in bulletins issued by the Ministry and the approval of the district authority is necessary for the purchase of books. The libraries are subsidized by provincial funds. Reading clubs for the purchase and circulation of magazines are suggested in the official regulations. Besides directing the reading the principal in charge of an extension course must also hold four conferences each year of those who must take part in further training. Lectures on educational subjects connected with the private reading, discussions of the curriculum, new methods and text-books, reports on the literature dealing with the elementary school, model lessons and addresses by specialists may form the work of these conferences. The participants must hand in an essay on some topic approved by the district inspector and the faculty of a normal school, which is corrected and returned at the succeeding conference and discussed. On the practical side the teacher must carefully perform his routine work, such as drawing up lesson-plans, dividing the annual course of study into sections for each month or half-month, and recording important parts of the work in a diary. The principal in charge of the further training visits them at their work and may inspect their diaries and other records and the exercise-books of their pupils.

The district inspectors and the principals in charge of extension courses conduct an annual conference for all teachers without exception.

The opportunities which the German teachers enjoy for further training in an informal way are numerous. They include

---

[9] Englmann, pp. 197-204.

teachers' associations, library facilities and educational museums, vacation courses at the universities and travel. The teachers' associations have developed a very great activity within the last decade. The earliest[10] efforts to realize a professional union among teachers arose in the eighteenth century out of conferences conducted by those of the clergy who recognized the importance of doing something to improve the type of teachers then offering themselves for service. At the beginning the work of assisting young teachers and particularly those who had not received training in a normal school was undertaken by older teachers at periodical conferences. Out of reading circles and associations for mutual assistance higher aims were evolved. The aim of the earliest societies was as much the improvement of public elementary education as of their members. Thus in 1805 there was formed the Society for the friends of the national school and educational system (*Gesellschaft der Freunde des vaterländischen Schul-und Erziehungswesens*), and in Berlin the Berlin School Society (1813) changed its title to Berlin School Association for German Elementary Education (*Berlinischer Schulverein für deutsches Volksschulwesen*).[11] As the professional consciousness rapidly increased teachers' festivals for teachers over a larger area began to be organized which met only for social purposes, but did not fail to contribute to an improvement of the professional standards and tone of those who attended. During the period of political awakening suspicion began to fall on the assemblies, conferences and associations of teachers. In 1842 the Rhenish Teachers were forbidden to hold their annual meeting; in 1843 the same prohibition was issued against the teachers of Silesia. But the opposition only served to strengthen the professional aspirations of the teachers. Their activity in connection with the Revolution of 1848 and the resolutions framed at Frankfort have already been referred to. A suggestion for a general association of teachers throughout Germany had been made in 1847, but the time was unpropitious.[12] In 1848, however, at a meeting of three hundred teachers held at Eisenach the General German Teachers' Association (*Allge-*

---

[10]For a full account of the subject of teachers' associations see Rissmann, Geschichte des deutschen Lehrervereins (Berlin, 1908).

[11]Rissmann, p. 23.

[12]Ibid., p. 43.

meine deutsche Lehrerverein) was formed, but met with so much opposition from the authorities in the different states that the permanent organization was changed in 1852 and its place was taken by a biennial conference (*Allgemeine deutsche Lehrerversammlung*).[13] Questions of method and general educational theory, matters affecting the professional status of elementary school teachers and the welfare of the schools, and opposition to clerical bureaucratic control formed the subjects of discussion. But the lack of some form of definite organization to represent the teachers was felt and in 1871 steps were taken to remedy this deficiency. In that year the German Teachers' Association (*Deutsche Lehrerverein*) was formed. The first aim of this association was declared to be to promote the progress of popular education through improvement of the elementary school. The association was to be distinctly undenominational. It also stood for better facilities and improvement in the training of teachers and for the economic welfare of its members. In organization it consists of local associations which subscribe to its statutes, and have no religious distinctions for membership. The association has made arrangements for the insurance of its members at reduced rates, provides legal aid, subsidizes a convalescent home for teachers, distributes information on matters affecting the teachers' interests, supports the *Deutsche Schulmuseum* at Berlin and the *Comenius-stiftung* in Leipzig, collects and publishes statistics, and issues a monthly journal (*Deutsche Schule*), and an annual (*Jahrbuch des deutschen Lehrervereins*). Like other associations the General German Association had its periods of difficulty. In 1880 it encountered the opposition of the Minister of Education, Puttkamer, who forbade teachers to attend its meetings. But succeeding ministers have recognized its importance. For a time it also had to contend against the opposition of the General Conference, but in 1893 the two were amalgamated. That an organization which stands for undenominationalism and professional inspection of schools should have incurred the suspicions of the reactionaries is not a matter for surprise. Opposition on this side led to the organization of denominational associations, the one representing protestant interests (*Verbande deutscher evangelischer Schul-und Lehrer-*

[13]Ibid., pp. 67-104.

vereine), and the other catholic (*Katholische Lehrerverband Deutschlands*). But the General Association has remained practically unaffected by these movements as may be seen from the fact that out of 124,027 teachers in the elementary schools 112,768 belonged to the Association in 1906. Of a more serious consequence is the recent movement among school principals to form an association devoted to their own interests and for the purpose of extending their powers in the schools and of demanding an increase of salary. This movement called out another to safeguard the interests of class-teachers. It is probable, however, that the excellent spirit shown by the principals in Berlin of forming a section within the General Association will contribute to a settlement of the matter and prevent any dissipation of the power of a body which can claim to represent the interests of almost the whole of the German teaching profession engaged in elementary schools.

Within the General Association there are smaller associations representing areas of smaller size. The chief of these is the Prussian Teachers' Association. But the larger the association, the more extensive and general is the scope of the topics which are discussed. It is in the local and necessarily small societies that an activity which is of importance for the professional growth of the teachers is developed. One association will be taken as a type and the syllabi of two of the branch societies will be given by way of example. The District Association of Hannover had twenty-four branch societies in 1908, each of which had on an average ten meetings during one year. At Hameln the following lectures[14] and discussions took place in the society which has a membership of thirty-nine, all the teachers of the town but one:

Lectures: 1. The danger of alcohol. 2. Animal psychology. 3. Heredity. 4. The origin of coal. 5. History of the origin of the earth. 6. Interest as the chief factor in education and instruction. 7. A lesson out of the industrial and handicrafts instruction in the local elementary school. 8. Sense-perception and idea. 9. Bacteriology in the elementary school. *Discussions:* The movement for equal pay. Report of the resolutions of dele-

---

[14]Taken from an announcement of the Bezirkslehrerverein, Hannover, 1908.

gates of the district on the salary question. The establishment of central treasuries for salaries. Support for young widows of teachers. Attitude on the inquiry of the mayor on the establishment of a public library and reading-room. Report on the annual district conference. The proposals of another local association on a reform of religious instruction.

At Polle where the association had a membership of nine out of ten local teachers the following programme represents activity for 1908:

Lectures: 1. Some theories of the origin of coral islands and coral reefs and their importance in geophysical questions. 2. Reform movements in the teaching of natural history. 3. How can the teacher aid in the relief of stuttering and stammering? 4. Modern lyric poetry. 5. A bacteriological study. 6. Apperception. 7. Mechanical difficulties in reading German script.

As an example of the assistance which the associations in the larger towns can afford to their members in their efforts for further education the excellent precedent established by the Teachers' Association of Leipzig may be cited. In 1906 there was founded by this Association the Institute for Experimental Pedagogy and Psychology (*Institut für experimentelle Pädagogik und Psychologie*), under the direction of Privatdozent Dr. Brahn.[15] The purpose of this institute is to teach its members the method of experimental pedagogy and psychology and to encourage experimental research in these fields. There is an annual introductory course in which the methods and the use of apparatus for experiment in psychology are taught. After this course monthly meetings are held for discussions, at which the following subjects have been treated: Individual differences, fatigue, children's drawings, the works of Meumann, the most suitable age for children to enter school. In another course the works on child study in English are translated and a study of Wundt's "Psychology" is made. In this connection should be mentioned that a translation of E. A. Kirkpatrick's "Fundamentals of Child Study " was made under the auspices of the Leipzig Teachers' Association. The following studies have been made as part of the research work conducted by the Institute:

---

[15]Kalender des Pestalozzi-Vereins (supplement), (Klinkhardt, Leipzig 1908)

The influence of question on the answer, the effect of sensations and emotions on pulsation and breathing in the case of healthy and pathological subjects, the perception of simple geometrical forms, the comprehension of number, the development of the color-sense in children, the psychology of children's drawings.

The Institute also conducts a special course in connection with the university extension classes, which are held annually under the auspices of the Saxon Teachers' Association. The course which lasts two weeks includes lectures on the following subjects: Meaning and purpose of sociology; ideation and memory; German literature; political economy; economic geography of Saxony; zoology; geology; experimental psychology. The course is open to all teachers, male and female, without distinction of residence or religion.

In those towns, however, which do not stand in such intimate relationship with universities the practice has grown up by which lecturers from neighboring universities conduct short courses under the auspices of the local teachers' associations.[16]

Two other means of self-improvement stand at the disposal of the German teachers, the libraries and educational museums. The library facilities are perhaps unexcelled. In addition to the local and district libraries, which in Prussia and Bavaria receive state subsidies, the teachers may obtain books from the national libraries at Berlin and Dresden, the *Deutsche Schulmuseum* in Berlin and the *Comenius Stiftung* in Leipzig, all of which distribute books by mail without charge. The museums play an important part, particularly in Prussia where they are largely used by teachers in preparation for the examinations for teachers in middle schools and school principals. The majority of the museums originated with the teachers' associations, which still control them, although several have been taken over by municipal corporations, while others receive government aid. The aim and purpose of the educational museums cannot be expressed better than in the statement of the City School Museum of Breslau. "To assist the teaching body of Breslau and the province in their further education and especially in their preparation for examinations, to aid the municipal authorities in the provision of suitable school appliances and equipment, and to afford advice and help

---

[16]Lexis, Vol. III, p. 323.

to every one who desires professional information, that is the aim of the Breslau school museum."[17] The chief sections of the museum include exhibits illustrating school architecture and furniture, school hygiene and statistics, teaching appliances, scientific collections, library, autographs, busts and portraits of important schoolmen.

While the other educational museums of Germany do not cover completely the scope of the Breslau museum in extent either of aim or collections, similar features are found in all of them. Thus the *Comenius-Stiftung* in Leipzig and the *Deutsche Schulmuseum* have educational libraries of considerable size and note; the *Städtische Schulmuseum* in Berlin in addition to a large library also possesses good laboratories to enable the teachers of the town to perform practical experiments in physics and chemistry in connection with which courses are also given at the museum; the museum at Magdeburg affords the teachers an opportunity of becoming acquainted with good school equipment and teaching appliances; the *Städtische Schulmuseum* in Hannover contains good physical and chemical cabinets, and collections of specimens for nature study and mineralogy.[18]

But however extensive the provisions for self-improvement through library and museum facilities and through short lecture courses may be, the demands of the whole of the German teachers engaged in elementary schools for opportunity to study at the universities continue to be vigorously agitated. Educators who are so well acquainted with the problems of teacher-training as Rein, Seyfert, Muthesius and Andreae, while they recognize the immediate impossibility of training teachers for the elementary schools at the universities, agree in supporting the demands for after-training in those institutions. The success of the experiment of granting the permission in Saxony, Hesse, Saxe-Weimar, and since 1906 in Bavaria, no longer justifies the opposition of the Prussian government in withholding university privileges from teachers in that state. The opposition is based mainly on the fear that teachers who have enjoyed university training would refuse to return to service in the elementary schools or at any

[17]Hübner, Das städtische Schulmuseum zu Breslau.

[18]Hübner, Die deutsche Schulmuseen (Breslau, 1904); Andrews, B. R., Museums of Education and their Uses, *Teachers College Record*, Sept. 1908 (New York, 1908).

rate in the rural schools, and that this course might eventually necessitate such a revision of the salary schedules as the state could not support. In addition to the opponents who belong to the reactionary camp and would refuse to see any improvement in the status of teachers, there are also those who are opposed to the admission of any students to the universities who have not a knowledge of Latin. A third form of opposition starts from the standpoint that as at present constituted the universities are not suitable institutions for the further training of teachers, and that until chairs in pedagogy and practice or experimental schools are established in all the universities, the teachers would receive no advantage from university privileges. But the probability of the removal of this deficiency in Prussia seems remote, and the study of education will for some time to come continue to be a part of the faculty of philosophy.[19]

Technically all who have pursued studies leading up to the privilege of military service of one year as a volunteer may matriculate at the universities for four to six semesters[20] (*kleine Immatrikulation*) without proceeding to a degree, but since there is another regulation forbidding those who are in the service of the state from being enrolled in the universities, all that remains to the graduates of the normal schools is the permission to attend lectures as auditors. The German, however, is dissatisfied with any course of study which does not conclude with some final examination and a diploma, so that little use is made of this privilege. University extension courses for teachers are held at the following universities: Berlin, Bonn, Breslau, Erlangen, Heidelberg, Kiel, Königsberg, Leipzig, Munich, and Würzburg. The nature of the course at Leipzig has already been described.

To Saxony[21] belongs the credit of first throwing open the university of Leipzig to elementary school teachers. The original grant of this privilege, which was first made in 1865, has since been somewhat restricted. At first permission to enter the university was given to those teachers who had obtained the first

---

[19]On the general question of University training of teachers see *Pädagogisches Jahrbuch*, 1905, pp. 175-181; 1906, pp. 139-147; 1907, pp. 202-205.

[20]*Pädagogisches Jahrbuch*, 1906, p. 146.

[21]*Leipziger Lehrerzeitung*, July 28, 1909, Das Universätsstudium der Sächsischen Seminarakademiker in den Grundzügen seiner bisherigen Entwickelung.

mark in the eligibility examination, while those who had only obtained the second mark could obtain permission by direct application to the ministry. Since 1890, however, the ministry will only consider applications from those who received the first mark with some qualification (Ib), and will only grant permission under special circumstances. Those who are admitted to the University under this regulation now have full university privileges and may proceed to a degree, but they are registered as students of pedagogy (*Kandidat der Pädagogik*), and must take academic subjects. To this examination reference has already been made as also to the privileges which it confers. The already been made as also to the privileges which it confers. The success of the students who avail themselves of this opportunity of attending the university has been frequently quoted to justify the extension of similar privileges to the Prussian teachers. The following comparative table showing the success in the degree examination of the fully matriculated students and those admitted under the law of 1865,[22] is significant, if some allowance is made for the influences of selection in both groups:

DISSERTATIONS

NORMAL SCHOOL GRADUATES

I (*egregia*)	II (*admodum*)	III (*laudabilis*)	IV (*idonea laudabil s*)
7 (15.2 per cent.)	23 (50 per cent.)	16 (34.8 per cent.)	. . . .

STUDENTS FULLY ADMITTED

| 45 (9.9 per cent.) | 174 (38.4 per cent.) | 183 (40.4 per cent.) | 51 (13.3 per cent.) |

ORAL EXAMINATIONS

NORMAL SCHOOL GRADUATES

I (*summa cum laude*)	II (*magna cum laude*)	III (*cum laude*)	IV (*rite laude*)
14 (30.4 per cent.)	23 (50 per cent.)	9 (19.6 per cent.)	. . . .

STUDENTS FULLY ADMITTED

| 72 (15.9 per cent.) | 186 (41 per cent.) | 148 (32.7 per cent.) | 47 (10.4 per cent.) |

[22]*Pädagogisches Jahrbuch*, 1905, p. 179.

These figures are compiled from the reports of the school of philosophy for the years 1900 to 1903. Whatever significance they have can, however, only be of value in Saxony. The difference between the training which is given in the Prussian and Saxon normal schools is so great, that it is doubtful whether the graduates of Prussian normal schools would make so good a showing. Of greater importance as an argument against those who fear that once the privilege of attending the university is granted to teachers there will be a general invasion, is the fact that in the summer semester of 1909 only one hundred and sixty-nine "students of pedagogy" were registered at Leipzig.

Since 1906 those teachers who pass an especially good examination on leaving the normal schools of Bavaria[23] may receive permission after two years' service to enter a university for two years. The course is to be concluded by an examination which will take the place of the appointments examination. It is very probable that from these students the future teachers will be selected for the normal schools. In the same year on the suggestion of Dr. Andreae, the minister of education, was induced to consult the three state universities on the advisability of establishing chairs of pedagogy and practice schools. Only one university, Erlangen, favored the establishment of a new chair of philosophy with the object of dealing with pedagogy. The replies on the other question were unfavorable. Pedagogy will for a further period remain to be treated by the professor of philosophy who may have the inclination to do so.[24]

At present the university of Jena continues to be the only institution where there is a model school for experimental work. To the pedagogical course teachers from all parts of Germany are admitted, but the study of pedagogy is taken up as a minor in the faculty of philosophy.

One other course remains for those who wish to study at the universities, but have not the requisite qualifications for entrance. By dint of private study they may make up the requirements for the *Abiturienten-examen* by passing which they can become fully registered students at the universities. The examination, however, is more rigorous for candidates who do not

---

[23] *Pädagogische Jahresschau*, 1906, p. 125 (Leipzig and Berlin, 1907).
[24] *Rept. U. S. Com. Educ.*, 1909, p. 500.

present themselves from the secondary schools after the recognized course of study. Private tutorial institutions exist for the purpose of cramming candidates for the examination. It may, however, be mentioned that teachers are warned against this method of approaching the universities.

Of travelling as a means of self-improvement the German teacher does not fail to avail himself. There are indications which show that his wanderings are taking him beyond the borders of his native country. The German Teachers' Association publishes a travellers' handbook every two years in the interest of its members.[25]

---

[25]Rissmann, p. 178.

CHAPTER IX

THE TRAINING OF WOMEN TEACHERS

The rapid and normally maintained increase of women teachers in Germany is demanding greater attention to what is becoming an important educational problem each year. Although the proportion of women to men has not reached and is not likely for some time to reach the figures in France, England and America, considerable alarm is felt at what is regarded as a rapid feminization of the elementary schools. While at one time the men were willing to permit the appointment of women to classes containing only girls, their encroachment into the lower mixed classes has been so great, that the views of men as expressed at teachers' associations are becoming unfavorable even to the limited appointment of women. The argument against the employment of women in schools in Germany takes the following lines: Education is a function shared by the schools with the family; in the latter the feminine influence is so strong that it must be balanced by the influence of men in the class-room. Even in the teaching of girls it has not been demonstrated that women are more qualified than men. Statistics are produced to prove that the employment of women is not efficient from the administrative point of view, for women are not physically adapted to resist the strain of the class-room and are consequently absent more frequently. In the last resort men teachers recognize a danger to the state in the increased employment of women. On the other hand there are many who not only support the appointment of women to girls' classes, but claim for them equal pay for equal work. At the same time the demand is made that women should receive the same training as men.

The facts, however, show that the increase of women teachers is inevitable and must be faced in Germany as in all other countries. Conditions at present favor the increase of women in the teaching profession, or at any rate are such as to favor the entrance of men into other occupations, owing to the general commercial prosperity of the country. The recent dearth of male teachers was a further factor favoring not only the increased employment of women, but in a part of Prussia even the suspension by Minister Studt of the rule against the appointment of married women. The Prussian salary law of 1909 gave the same increase of initial salary to women and men.

The following table[1] shows the number of women teachers in the three representative states and the comparative increase in five years, 1901-1906:

	WOMEN TEACHERS		INCREASE	INCREASE OF MEN	PER CENT. OF WOMEN IN PROFESSION	
	1901	1906	*Per cent.*	*Per cent.*	1901	1906
Prussia.....	13,866	17,784	28.3	11.3	15	17
Bavaria.....	2,715	3,861	42.2	3.1	18	24
Saxony.....	401	653	62.8	20.6	4	5

In the same period the increase in the number of school children attending the elementary schools of Prussia was 8.72 per cent. and of girls alone approximately 1.5 per cent.[2] Thus the increase of women teachers in Prussia in the five years has been absolute. It must be added that the greater part of the increase occurred in Catholic districts not only through the female teaching orders but also through the large number of lay women inspired by them to enter the teaching profession.[3]

The training of women teachers in Prussia has not received the same attention as the training of men. With the exception of the regulations governing the Royal Normal School for Women Teachers in Droyssig no other regulations have been published. The Droyssig regulations, however, furnish a standard for the other normal schools. There are fifteen royal normal schools for women and forty-five established by cities, usually in connection with a higher school for girls. At Droyssig candidates must be between seventeen and twenty-four at the time of entering. The

[1]*Pädagogisches Iahrbuch*, 1907, p. 232.
[2]*Statistisches Jahrbuch für den preussischen Staat*, 1908, p. 157.
[3]Herber, Das Lehrerinnenwesen in Deutschland, p. 117.

entrance examination which is written and oral includes a written German essay and some problems in arithmetic, and oral questions similar to those given to candidates for entrance to the normal schools for men. A knowledge of French, singing, piano or violin is expected. In those normal schools which are attached to higher girls' schools candidates enter the normal schools on completing the high school course. The curriculum of the normal schools is regulated by the requirements of the examination for women teachers of April 24th, 1874.[4]

In addition to the royal and city normal schools there are also numerous private institutions which serve to prepare candidates for the teachers' examination. The result of this indiscriminate preparation was to cause the issue of a regulation in 1901[5] by which all candidates who presented themselves for examination must produce evidence of having had practical training.

The training of women teachers is somewhat complicated in Prussia by the fact that in the majority of normal schools candidates for appointment in the elementary and higher girls' schools follow the same courses. In fact it may be said that the majority of girls commence with the intention of entering service in the higher institutions and that frequently the elementary school is an afterthought due to failure to pass the examination for employment in the higher girls' schools. The duration of the normal school courses for women is three years. The candidates are in most cases better prepared than those who enter the normal schools for men. The majority on entering have already enjoyed a secondary education in a school which did not prepare exclusively for the normal schools. Thus a good knowledge of German, French and English, history and geography can be expected. But the same standard will not have been attained in mathematics as by the men. In science and religion there is no perceptible difference. So far as academic preparation is concerned the women students in the normal schools have a better start than the men, in so far as their preparation has not been limited by restricted requirements.

The curriculum consists of the following subjects: German, religion, mathematics, history, geography, needlework, French

---

[4]Bremen, p. 297.
[5]Ibid, p. 305.

and English, nature study (including some physics and chemistry), drawing, gymnastics, music and pedagogy. The last subject is divided into history of education, psychology and educational theory and is spread over the three years of the course. The method of each subject is taught by the instructor in charge of the subject. The theoretical part of the professional work is given as much attention as in the men's normal schools. The training is weak on the practical side. Observation and practice are not taken up until the third year and take place usually in the lower classes of the girls' higher schools. Each student has from six to eight hours of observation and practice during each week, of which about two are devoted to practice. The class-teacher is always present, and frequently several students. Very commonly each practising student teaches only for half a period. The lessons are discussed beforehand and it is then decided whether one or more students shall teach during the period. In no case do the student-teachers have full charge of the class, as for example in the control of the books and discipline. A further defect is that the teacher of method is very rarely present during the practice-lessons in his subjects. As a rule the student-teachers in the women's normal schools are lacking in initiative, and often do little else than imitate a lesson which they have observed.

A reform[6] of the entire system of training women teachers is, however, in progress and it is very probable that more attention will be paid to practice-teaching in the future. The proposed reform is designed to extend the course by an additional year. The first three years will be devoted to academic and the fourth to purely professional training. At the same time it is also likely that the training of candidates for elementary and girls' higher schools will be differentiated, although at present the only additional, but not required, work which is carried by the student who intends to enter an elementary school is English.

With the exception of the practice work the standards in the women's normal schools seem higher than in those for men. Of course there is a better foundation when the candidates enter the normal schools, and the pressure is considerably less, but in addition there is an utter absence of the drill and recitation method

[6] *Central-Blatt*, April, 1909, p. 370.

which is so marked in the normal schools for men. There is more cooperation and activity in the class-room and a higher standard of scholarship. The language lessons attain a very high level of perfection and are always taught by instructors who have studied the languages abroad. The whole of the lessons are carried on without a word of German. So far as English is concerned the only criticism one could pass is that the readers apart from the works of Shakespere by no means impressed one as classics.

At the end of the three years candidates, if they have reached the age of nineteen, may present themselves for examination. A certain number of schools have the privilege of setting their own leaving examinations, which are recognized by the state as qualifying for appointment. Where this privilege does not hold, candidates must present themselves for examination before a commission consisting of a commissioner representing the provincial school board and three or more members appointed by the Chief President of the province and consisting of school councillors and directors and instructors of girls' higher schools. The examination is theoretical and practical. The theoretical examination is written and oral. The written part consists of a German essay, some problems in arithmetic, and a French exercise. The theory and practice of education, and the obligatory subjects of the elementary school form the subjects of the oral test. The practical examination consists of the presentation of a lesson for the preparation of which twenty-four hours are allowed. The marks, which are given on the examination as a whole, are "very good," "good," "satisfactory" and "unsatisfactory," the last being equivalent to failure.[7]

Women teachers like the men are appointed provisionally, but unlike the men they are not required to pass a second examination for permanent appointment. At the end of two years at the earliest and not later than five years from their first appointment, they may be confirmed in their positions, provided that their work in service warrants such a course. After five years' service the examination for women school principals[8] (of girls' schools, elementary, middle and higher) may be taken. This consists of an essay which the candidates prepare in eight weeks,

[7]Bremen, p. 297 ff.
[8]Ibid., p. 303.

and an oral examination in the history and principles of education, psychology, special method, a knowledge of school appliances and popular and child literature. There are also special examinations for women teachers of female handicrafts, drawing and gymnastics, in which courses of instruction are offered, similar to those which are open to men.

As was mentioned earlier women teachers were originally confined to classes containing only girls and later to lower mixed classes. Although these restrictions are gradually disappearing, a position once held by a man cannot be filled by a woman without a formal change of the character of that position.[9]

The training of women in Saxony and Bavaria shows very little variation from that of the men. In Saxony[10] there are only three normal schools for women (Callnberg, Dresden and Leipzig). The duration of the courses is four or five years. The entrance qualifications consist of a knowledge of the work of a graded elementary school, although credit is given for work done beyond that stage. These normal schools differ from those for men in substituting English for Latin, but this subject as well as music is optional; while French and needlework are compulsory. The qualifying examinations for appointment are the same as for the men. Women are not exempted from further examinations for permanent appointment. So far as the nature of their appointments are concerned women may only be employed in girls' classes or in mixed classes in the lower or middle sections of schools. As in Prussia women teachers can only hold their appointments until marriage.

The training of women teachers for elementary schools in Bavaria[11] is left to private institutions with the exception of three state normal schools. The course of training in the state institutions is similar to that for men with the substitution of French and female handicrafts for agriculture, and preparation for secretarial and church service. Instruction in music is limited to singing and the violin. Each of the three state normal schools (Munich, Memmingen and Aschaffenburg) is governed by special regulations. Candidates on entering the preparatory

---

[9]Plüschke, p. 178.

[10]Kretzschmar, J. F., pp. 92-100.

[11]Englmann, pp. 439 ff.

sections must be between the ages of thirteen and seventeen, and must pass an examination in the subjects of a graded elementary school. The preparatory course extends over three years, at the end of which candidates on passing an examination in the work of the third year may enter on the two-year normal school course. All candidates whether trained in a public or private institution must pass the final examination of a public normal school before they can enter on the practical training preparatory to employment as teachers (*Schuldienst-exspectantinnen*). At the end of four years they may present themselves for the appointments examination (*Anstellungsprüfung*), which has already been described. Women can only be appointed to positions previously held by women or to schools where one or more men teachers are employed. In every case they may only teach classes of girls or mixed classes in the lower sections. The appointments held by women lapse on their marriage.

In addition to lay women teachers a large number of women belonging to teaching orders is employed in Bavaria. These teachers must have the ordinary qualifications. They are only employed by consent of town or district authorities, who enter into agreements with the superior of the order for the supply of teachers and the salaries to be paid. The responsibility of appointment then rests with the superior and the approval of the usual administrative authority is not required.

The salaries of women teachers are in Prussia and Bavaria lower than those for men. But the appointments carry with them the provision of a house or compensation for rent and the right to pensions. In Prussia the initial salary for women teachers not holding a permanent appointment is 960 M. ($240); this rises on definite appointment to 1200 M. ($300). The increments which begin after seven years' service and accrue every three years are for the first two payments 100 M. ($25) and 150 M. ($37.50) thereafter. Pensions are paid in the same proportions to women as to men.[12]

The initial salary of an assitant schoolmistress (*Hilfslehrerin*) in Bavaria[13] is 820 M. ($205) a year rising on permanent appointment to 1000 M. ($250). The first increment after five

---

[12]*Das Lehrerbesoldungsgesetz vom.* 26 *Mai,* 1909.
[13]Englmann, p. 210.

years' service is 72 M. ($18), followed by four increments of 48 M. ($12) and four of 60 M. ($15) at intervals of five years. On retiring from service women teachers are assured a minimum pension of 720 M. ($180) a year.

In Saxony the salary scales are the same for men and women so far as the minima assured by the state are concerned.

A comparison[14] of the service ages of men and women teachers in Prussia is adequate testimony to the fact that women have entered the profession to stay, although the sudden drop shown by the first two figures is evidence as much of the lack of physical endurance as of the presence of other opportunities. On the whole, however, the comparison is very favorable for the women:

YEARS OF SERVICE	MEN	WOMEN
	Per cent.	Per cent.
Up to five	19.47	31.92
From 6-10	17.99	21.61
11-15	15.17	14.10
16-20	15.19	12.60
21-30	18.98	15.78
31-39	10.03	3.54
40-49	3.04	.44
50 and over	.13	.01

The sudden drop after thirty years of service is explicable on the ground that women did not enter either the teaching or other occupations in such large numbers thirty years ago, although inability to stand the strain may be largely responsible for the dropping-out at this period as well as in the first ten years of service.

Within the last twenty years associations[15] of women teachers have developed great activity. The most important of these is the *Allgemeine deutsche Lehrerinnenverein,* which is undenominational. One of the elements of strength in the movement is that teachers of all grades of schools have up to the present stood together. The probability, however, is that the near future will see the development of new societies along class distinctions, fos-

[14]Herber, p. 121.
[15]Ibid., pp. 162 ff.

tered by the regulation for the separation of the training of teachers for girls' higher and elementary schools. The General Association of Women Teachers (*Allg. d. Lehrerinnenverein*) was founded in 1890 to promote the intellectual and material welfare of women teachers, and to advance the interests of popular education. The association has committees for social work, legal protection, the collection of statistics, and for propaganda. Since the association is open not only to those engaged in teaching but to all women, it has become the centre of the women's movement in Germany and has brought out some of the most able leaders among the German women of the present.

In addition to the General Association several denominational societies exist.

There can be no doubt that the employment of women in schools will continué to increase in Germany, but it is difficult to say how long it will be before conditions reach the same position as in other countries. Certain it is that the progress of the movement for the emancipation of women has proportionately been more rapid in Germany within the last fifteen years than elsewhere. Whether the self-interest of the male teaching body together with an unreasoning prejudice or conviction that the employment of women teachers is dangerous to the welfare of the state will be powerful enough to prevent the increase of women in the teaching profession remains to be seen. But it may be said with some degree of certainty that the men have not made out a case for their claim that they understand the problem of teaching girls better than their female colleagues. So long as the separation of the sexes continues to be maintained in the schools of Germany, so long will the claim of the women to more increased employment in the teaching of girls be justified.

CHAPTER X

SUMMARY AND CONCLUSIONS

Germany insists that the teachers of the country shall be trained. For this purpose a training course of six years has been established. The training institutions are segregated from other types of education so that specialization may be said to begin with the fourteenth year. The first three years of the course are preparatory and academic; the last three years are academic and professional. Practical work is begun in the fifth year and continued through the last year, the amount varying in the different states. The graduates of the normal schools are only appointed on probation. In order to secure permanent appointments candidates must undergo a second examination, consisting mainly of professional subjects. While female teachers are in a minority, their number is rapidly increasing. In many states they enjoy the same training as the men, but in Prussia the system of training young women is not yet definitely determined.

It is a matter of some difficulty in attempting to estimate the value of an educational system in a foreign country to decide on the standards of criticism to be adopted. And this is particularly true in a consideration of the German system from an American or English standpoint. On the one side are monarchy, direction, systematization, the most stringent form of bureaucratic control. On the other side are found democracy, local control, an almost complete absence of system, or almost as many systems as there are normal schools. Differences of nationality, of environment, of traditions mean differences of ideals and method of attainment. It would be well perhaps to go back to the question of the motives which prompt society to establish public schools. The primary motive is the desire of society to realize its ideals through the schools and the instrumentality of the teachers. Judged by this standard the German system of training teachers, the first step towards the realization of the German ideals, is highly successful. The aim of the elementary school in Germany is to impart to the pupils a reverence for authority, human and divine, and a certain amount of knowledge. With this goes the acceptance of a fixed and definite amount of intellectual attainments suitable for the masses of the nation. Such an aim, since it is definite and precise, it must be admitted is not difficult to attain. The case is different with America. Here the ideal, while generally recognized and accepted as the true ideal of a democratic people, is vague and expressed in terms which as yet have no definite content. The encouragement of individuality, the equalization of opportunity, training for social efficiency are complex terms which easily lend themselves to discussion without providing an answer to the question of how they are to be attained. This vagueness and complexity added to the necessity of adapting to local circumstances have been causes of the slow progress made by the American normal schools. The success of the German system, and it is permissible to talk of a system since the whole of Germany upholds the ideal mentioned above, lies in the careful organization of means to realize a well-defined end. This is a lesson which the American normal schools cannot neglect. The problem is difficult and complicated but on its solution and on the establishment of a national standard depend the successful organization and administration of the normal schools, and the ultimate success of elementary education.

But while the German system illustrates the importance of realizing the end to be attained, it is an equally good example of the dangers of centralized administration and bureaucratic control. To these causes is due the fact that there is a monotonous similarity among the normal schools of one state. Neither the director nor the instructor is permitted to depart from the prescription of the central authority. The individuality of the instructors as much as of the pupils is sacrificed to the necessities of the administrative regulations. Uniformity is attained, but it is the undeviating uniformity of a machine. The national aim is placed above all else; local needs and local variations are disregarded. At the other extreme stands the American practice, which is characterized by great variations, absence of national standards and a certain amount of local adaptation. But while such variation, if intelligently directed, affords opportunities for experimentation, leading ultimately to higher standards, there is a danger that local needs may prove too strong for the maintenance of requirements which are generally considered desirable in a teacher. Hence it is impossible to talk of a system; hence the qualifications of teachers differ from one state to another, from one county to another in the same state, and from one city to another. The teachers of one state system may differ according to the grade of certificate that they hold and the previous training which they have received. It is significant that each local system until recently tended to hedge itself in and refuse to recognize the certification of its neighbor.[1] In Prussia, however, a teacher from one part of the state can fit naturally into any type of elementary school in another part, and throughout Germany a certain amount of recognition of interstate certification is provided for. In that country the teacher is a person with qualifications which have a definite and widely understood significance; in this country the qualifications may have been obtained by examination in common school branches, in normal school with a course of any number of years after the elementary or high school, which in turn is not standardized, or lastly in a college, equally vague and undefined. The importance of a standardization of requirements has long been recognized in Germany; the growth of a national system of education will be retarded in this country until the same recognition is given to this need. At the same time, however, the German system may serve as a warning against centralization. But the recognition of the same standards is not incompatible with local administrative freedom and the exercise of initiative by the directors of normal schools. The English practice is a happy illustration of such a system in operation. There the central Board of Education has established a lower limit in the training of teachers and publishes courses of study. The principals of normal schools are at liberty to accept the suggestions for the curriculum issued by the Board or to frame their own programmes, provided that this accords with the requirements of the central authority and an adequate reason for the departure can be given. Under such a system it is pos-

---

[1]See Cubberly, Certification of Teachers, Ch. VIII (Chicago, 1906).

sible to have side by side denominational and non-sectarian training colleges, local systems of training teachers and university departments of education, all meeting the requirements of the Board and at the same time exercising a certain amount of individual responsibility. As a further illustration of the elasticity of the system it may be mentioned that candidates may qualify for the certificate of the Board without attending any training college. While on this topic a further point of contrast between the English and German systems may be mentioned, as it is suggestive for American practice. Within recent years there has been a prolongation of the preparation through the secondary schools of those who intend to enter the teaching profession, to which is now added a year's experience as a student-teacher. Without entering into the merits of this previous training through apprenticeship, which depends so largely on the ability of the headmaster to whom the student is assigned, the principle by which a good academic training is given and too early specialization is avoided must be emphasized. The present situation in England is also helpful as an indication of the tendency to raise the standards of qualifications demanded from elementary school teachers. A regulation has already been carried by which in 1914 vaccination and the attainment of the eighteenth birthday will no longer be recognized as qualifications to teach the rising generation. There is no doubt that a general levelling of standards will take place in America in an upward direction as soon as the disparities in wealth and population between the states have been removed. This process will inevitably be slow, but changes and compromises can be made gradually as has been pointed out elsewhere.[2]

Another factor, however, enters into the problem of training teachers in America, which up to the present has only been making itself felt to a slight extent in Germany. There can be but little doubt that a good system of training teachers cannot be built up when the short period of their service not only adds to the expense of maintaining normal schools, but, owing to the need of keeping up a constant supply to fill the rapidly recurring vacancies, necessarily impairs efficiency. How the interplay of demand and supply affected the German normal schools was

[2]Cubberly, Certification of Teachers.

illustrated in the lowering of the standards in the entrance examinations a few years ago. But what was in Germany regarded as a more serious matter was the increased employment of women in the schools. The recent revision of salaries in Prussia and Saxony was an attempt to attract men back to the schools from the other and more remunerative occupations, for the feminization of the schools is generally viewed with alarm. But whether the situation is alarming or not, Germany must soon accept it as a fact as much as France, England and America. The problem of readjustment is likely to be difficult, but with the support of a national tradition and the centralized authority the female teacher will be able to carry out the task which is set before her. In a democratic state, however, there is something incongruous in placing a teacher, immature in years and experience, to teach the lessons and duties of a democratic citizen.

Up to this point the lessons which may be drawn from a study of the German administration in its relation to the teacher have been dealt with. Coming to the more narrow field it will be found that the German system of training has some suggestive ideas to offer. Not the least important of these is the Prussian practice of entrusting the teaching of subject-matter and methods, and the supervision of practice to the same instructor. Any divorce of these functions is likely to lead to friction on the one side and to confusion in the mind of the students on the the other. And yet the Saxon practice of separation most generally prevails in the American normal schools. Undoubtedly the difference in the number of pupils in the normal schools of the two countries leads to the differences in practice. The employment of critic teachers and directors of practice-teaching as distinct from the normal school instructors presupposes absolute unanimity among them to secure success. On the whole, however, the Prussian practice has more to recommend it than that which is more current here, although it is dangerous to generalize in this as in so many other questions concerning the American normal schools.

The different types of practice-teaching which are to be found in Germany have been considered. The chief defect seems to be an absence of sufficient preliminary observation of children. The main object of such observation as exists is to study the technique of the teacher. Here again the practice varies widely in

American schools, but it may be said generally that opportunities for the observation of children are provided without, in many cases, being directed. In both countries the necessity of supplying teachers able to take full control of classes has tended to lay the emphasis in the practice-work on the apprenticeship type. To this is added the recognition that the average length of service of the American teacher is short in any case. For the same reason, while the system of appointing teachers on probation for a period of from two to five years is suggestive, it would be difficult to enforce throughout this country. The system of recognizing certificates of different grades is not the same as a period of probation, because in the first place it militates against homogeneity, and secondly it gives the very inefficient teacher and the teacher who has other plans for the future an opportunity of obtaining an appointment at any rate for a few years. Nor is the renewal of certificates by means of examinations the best way of testing those qualities in a teacher which cannot be put down on paper. Under appropriate conditions, which it must be admitted do not as yet prevail in America, the most commendable plan for the practical preparation of the teacher would be the laboratory method of practice-teaching as recommended by Dewey[3] and a probationary period to select those who prove their ability to develop efficiency in the class-room.

The organization of the practice-schools in Prussia affords a highly valuable suggestion for American normal schools. An opportunity is afforded in most of the Prussian normal schools for the students to become acquainted with the type of school in which the majority will probably take up their work. While, however, this opportunity is confined to the acquisition of classroom technique in the ungraded school, it is possible to conceive how this might easily be utilized to bring out the more special problems of the rural school. In this country the demands of this type of schools are becoming more and more insistent and the sporadic attempts which are being made at present must eventually be more widely extended until a larger number of normal schools will be in a position to prepare their students to meet the problems of the rural community. In Prussia the drift of teachers to the city systems is checked by administrative regulations.

---

[3]Theory and Practice in the Training of Teachers.

Such a course is inconceivable in this country and must be replaced by instilling in the future teachers a genuine appreciation of rural conditions as well as by economic attractions.

It bears excellent testimony to the progress which this country has made in the science of education that in the field of elementary education Germany, her early teacher, has little to offer that is suggestive. The system which Mann, Stowe, Bache and others praised in the forties of the last century with so much enthusiasm, is still essentially the system of Germany to-day. The lessons which the early reformers wished to emphasize have been well learned, and even if they have been learned only in patches, the elements for further progress are within this country. And after all the problems which have to be faced are American, the conditions which education must meet are American, and the ideals which have to be realized are American. The solution, therefore, must be discovered on American soil. Other countries may offer suggestions on a point here or a point there. How far the German system of training teachers may prove of value to the question in this country it has been the purpose of this chapter to show.

While eminently successful in attaining their object, the German normal schools illustrate the dangers of applying bureaucratic methods in education. Superior authority and dictatorial methods are not calculated to develop initiative and personality, qualities which above all are desirable in a teacher.

APPENDIX

TABLE I

Time-Table in the Preparatory Courses

	Prussia			Saxony			Bavaria		
Religion	4	4	3	4	4	4	3	3	3
German	5	5	5	3(4)	3(4)	3(4)	6	6	6
Foreign Languages	3	3	3	7(6)	7(6)	5(4)	..	..	...
History	2	2	2	2	2	2	2	2	2
Mathematics	5	5	5	4	4	5	4	4	4
Natural Science	2	4	4	2	2	3	2	2	2
Geography	2	2	2	2	2	2	2	2	2
Writing	2	2	1	2	2	1	1	1	1
Drawing	2	2	3	2	2	2	3	3	3
Gymnastics	3	3	3	3	3	3	2	2	2
Music	3	4	5	5	4	3	6	6	6
Optional									
Piano	..	..	..	1	1	1	..	..	...
Stenography	..	..	..	..	..	2	2	2	2

TABLE II

Daily Routine in a Prussian Normal School

Week Days		Sunday	
5	Rise	6	Rise
5.30–6.15	Study	7	Breakfast
6.20	Breakfast	7.30	Prayers
6.50	Prayers	8–9	Free occupations
7–9.50	Class work	9–9.15	Second breakfast
9.50–10.05	Second breakfast	9.30	Church
10.10–12	Class work	12.10	Lunch
12.10	Lunch	12.30–6	Free
12–3	Free periods	3.50–4.10	Coffee
3–6	Class work or study	6–7	Free occupations
3.50–4.10	Coffee	7.10	Supper
7.10	Supper	8.15–9.15	Study
.15–9.15	Study	9.30	Prayers and bed
9.30	Prayers and bed		

On Wednesday and Saturday afternoons there are half-holidays.

TABLE III

OFFICIAL TIME-TABLES IN NORMAL SCHOOLS

	PRUSSIA			SAXONY			BAVARIA*e*	
Year of course.......	III	II	I	III	II	I	II	I
Pedagogy...........	3	3	3	4	5	5	4	4
Lesson planning and model lessons......	...	(4*a*)	4	...	...	...	...	....
Practice teaching.....	...	...	4–6	...	4	4	...	....
Religion............	3	4	3*b*	4	4	3	3	3
German.............	5	5	3*b*	3	4	3	4	4
Foreign languages....	2	2	2	4	2	2	...	....
History.............	2	2	2	2	2	2	2	2
Mathematics........	5	5	1*c*	4	4	3	3	3
Natural Science......	4	4	1	3	2	2	5	2
Geography..........	3	2	1*c*	2	2	...	1	1
Drawing............	2	2	1	2	1	1	2	2
Gymnastics.........	3	3	3*b*	3	2	2	2	2
Music..............	4	4	4	3*d*	3*d*	3*d*	6	6
Agriculture.........	1	1 { 1	...	...	...	...	...	....
Total..........	38	38	33–35	34	35	30	32	29

a Included with subject-matter.
b One hour for method.
c Method.
d Singing only; instrumental music optional.
e In addition, instruction is given in first year in church service, and in law in the second, one hour each.

Comparison of Some Smaller States with Prussia*

	Prussia	Weimar	Eisenach	Gotha	Altenburg	Rudolstadt
Number of classes with one year course.	6 classes: 3 Preparatory; 3 normal school. 30 students in a class.	6 classes. 25-30 students in a class.	6 classes: 3 Preparatory; 3 normal school. 30 students in a class.	6 classes, 22 students in a class.	6 classes. Under certain conditions pupils may enter any class for which they are ready. 30 students in a class.	6 classes. 20 students in a class.
Boarding or day school.	Either.	Day.	Day.	Either.	Either.	Boarding mainly.
Regulations for work and conduct.	Strict.	Moderate. Dramatic performances and concerts are held.	Moderate. Visit and cooperate at concerts.		Moderate. Senior students free up to 9 p.m.	Moderate. Senior students free to 10 p.m.
State support for students.	Liberal. No fees.	c 2000 M., 30 free places. Fees, 20 M.	c 1000-1500 M., 20 free places. 20 M., 5 free table-boarders.	2000 M. Fees.	Everything free; 50-70 M. in addition to each student.	Fees; and only 15 free table-boarders.
Pledge to serve.	For 5 years.	For 6 years.	For 6 years.		For 6 years.	Period not stated.
Entrance requirements: (1) Age.	14 years for preparatory; 17 years for normal school.	14 years. Graduates of Realschule may enter class IV under certain conditions.	17 years for normal school.	Students received in any class up to II. 14 years to enter lowest class.	14 years.	14 years.
(2) Certificates.	Good conduct and health; baptism	Same as Prussia.	Same as Prussia.	Same as Prussia.	Same as Prussia.	Same as Prussia.
(3) Intellectual standards.	For preparatory Common school subjects: Religion, German, history, arithmetic, geography.	Common school subjects.	Middle school subjects, with music and science, but no foreign language.	Common school subjects, music and beginnings of French	Common school subjects and music (piano, violin if possible.)	Common school subjects and music (piano and violin; organ if possible.)
Academic and professional subjects.	Academic to class II in normal school; class I largely professional.	Academic carried through; professional begun in class III.	As at Weimar.	As in Prussia.	Academic throughout; professional begin in III.	As in Prussia.
Periods of instruction.	31 in III and II of normal school.	31 in II.	28-29 in III and II.	30 in III and II.	33 in II in winter; 31 in II in summer.	31 in III and II.

Subjects of instruction in normal school:

Subject	Prussia III	II	I	Weimar III	II	I	Eisenach III	II	I	Gotha III	II	I	Altenburg III	II	I	Rudolstadt
Pedagogy	·	3	3	3	·	3	3	1	3	2-4	5	7	4	4	4	III
Methods and model lessons	·	4	4-6	·	·	2	·	5	·	·	·	·	·	·	4-6	As in Prussia, except Religion, which has: III 4, II 3, I 2
Practice	·	3	3	·	·	·	·	·	·	·	·	·	·	·	·	
Religion	5	5	3	3	3	3	3	3	3	4	4	·	·	·	4	
German	5	5	2	3	3	5	5	3	5	5	4	·	5	4	6	
Foreign language	2	2	2	2	2	2	·	2	·	2	2	2	2	2	2	
History	5	5	4	4	5	4	4	4	3	5	4	2	5	4	4	
Mathematics	4	4	3	3	2	3	3	3	3	4	4	1	4	4	·	
Natural Sciences	2	2	3	3	5	3	3	2	2	4	4	2	5	5	1	
Geography	2	2	3	3	4	3	3	2	2	2	2	2	2	2	2	
Drawing	4	4	3	3	3	3	3	2	2	2	2	·	3	3	2	
Gymnastics	2	2	3	3	2	2	2	2	2	4	4	·	5	5	4	
Music	3	3	4	6	6	6	7	2	7	1	1	1	2	2	2	
Agriculture	1	1	·	4	·	·	·	·	·	·	·	·	4-5	4-5	1	

*Adapted from Schmidt, A. M. Über den gegenwärtigen Stand der Lehrerbildung und Lehrerbildung in Thüringen; in *Mitteilungen des Vereins der Freunde Herbartischer Pädagogik* (Langensalza, 1907).

TABLE V

Typical Time Table of a Complete Training School in Prussia

	MONDAY				**TUESDAY**				**WEDNESDAY**			
		PRACTICE-SCHOOL				PRACTICE-SCHOOL				PRACTICE-SCHOOL		
	Normal School	Graded	Ungraded	Prepy. Inst.	Normal School	Graded	Ungraded	Prepy. Inst.	Normal School	Graded	Ungraded	Prepy. Inst.
7–8	I History III Religion Pedagogy	1a Religion 1b German 2,3 } Religion 4,5		Nature Study Religion Religion	German Mathematics History	1a German 1b 2,3 } Religion 4,5	Religion	French German Religion	Religion German Mathematics			History Religion German Arithmetic
8–9	I Organ II History III Drawing	1a German 1b Religion 2,3 } German 4,5	Religion	Geography German German	Drawing Gymnastics			Organ Geography German	Religion German	German	German	Drawing French
9–10	I Organ II Gymnastics III Drawing		German	Arithmetic German French	Drawing Mathematics		German	German Harmony Gymnastics	Mathematics Religion	1a German 1b 2,3 } Writing 4,5	German	Geography Drawing History
10–11	II Physics III Geography	Arithmetic	Arithmetic	History Nature Study Arithmetic	Chemistry German	Arithmetic		Singing History Arithmetic	Geography Pedagogy	1a Gymn'st's 1b Drawing 2,3 } History 4,5 } Gymnastics	History	German Nature Study Geography
11–12	I Religion II Mathematics III Natural Science			Biblical History Geography Geometry	Religion	Model Lessons		Nature Study Gymnastics Geometry	Harmony			
1–2		Nature Study	Nature Study			Drawing, Writing and Handwork						
2–3		History or Gymnastics	Gymnastics			Drawing, Writing and Handwork						
3–4	I Gymnastics II Singing III Singing	1a Geometry 2 (girls) } Handwork		Writing French	History French Natural Science	1a 1b } Geography 2,3	Geography	Gymnastics Violin Writing	Violin			
4–5	I German III Pedagogy III Violin			Gymnastics Music	French German French			Piano Writing Singing	Choral Singing			
5–6	I Pedagogy III Singing III Gymnastics			Music Music Violin	Pedagogy Organ			Violin Singing				
6–7	I Gymnastics II Organ				Violin							

TYPICAL TIME TABLE OF A COMPLETE TRAINING SCHOOL IN PRUSSIA

	THURSDAY				FRIDAY				SATURDAY			
	Normal School	Graded	Ungraded	Prepy. Inst.	Normal School	Graded	Ungraded	Prepy. Inst.	Normal School	Graded	Ungraded	Prepy. Inst.
7-8	History German German	} Religion	Religion	French German Religion	German Physics French	1a German } Religion	Religion	German Religion German	Mathematics German German	1a Religion } German	Religion	History Geometry Religion
8-9	History Geography	} Religion	Religion	Drawing French German	German Natural Science	Religion	Religion	Arithmetic History	Gymnastics Religion			Geography Religion Piano
9-10	Mathematics History	} German	German	Drawing Geography Arithmetic	Religion Geography	Religion } German		Geometry Organ French	Mathematics Pedagogy	Writing	German and Writing	French Geography Gymnastics
10-11	Drawing Religion	} Arithmetic	Arithmetic	German Arithmetic Nature Study	Pedagogy Geography	} Arithmetic		Harmony Religion Drawing	Geography Mathematics	History Writing Singing	History	Catechism Drawing Geography
11-12	Natural Science Mathematics			Biblical History Geometry Gymnastics	Organ	Model Lessons	Singing and Writing	Nature Study Nature Study Drawing	Singing	Gymnastics and Singing	Geometry and Reading	Writing and Drawing Writing Nature Study
1-2		1a 1b } Geography 2 3 4 5 } Writing	Geography			Singing	Singing and Writing					
2-3		History Gymnastics	Gymnastics			Nature Study	Nature Study					
3-4	Gymnastics	1a Geometry 1b German 3 (girls) Handwork	German	German Organ	French Harmony	1a Physics 1b German		Gymnastics Piano				
4-5	French Agriculture			Piano Writing	Religion Chemistry Violin			Violin Gymnastics				
5-6	Pedagogy Gymnastics Agriculture			Violin	Geography Harmony German			Violin				
6-7	Gymnastics				Conference Organ			Piano				

BIBLIOGRAPHY

History of the Training of Teachers in Germany

Barnard, H. German Teachers and Educators. Pestalozzi and Pestalozzianism.

Dinter. Autobiographie.

Fischer, K. Geschichte des deutschen Volksschullehrerstandes (Berlin, 1898).

Francke, A. W. Erinnerung an Studirende der Theologie, etc.; and other writings contained in Richter's edition.

Herber, Pauline. Das Lehrerinnenwesen in ·Deutschland (München, 1906).

Kehr, C. Die Geschichte des Schullehrerseminars zu Halberstadt, *Pädagogische Blätter*, 1878.

Kreitz, W. Diesterweg und die Lehrerbildung, eine Geschichte der deutschen Lehrerbildung (Wittenberg, 1890).

Leuschke, A. Zur Geschichte der Lehrerbildungsfrage im Königreich Sachsen (Dresden, 1904).

Mertz, G. Das Schulwesen der deutschen Reformation (Heidelberg, 1902).

Rissmann, R. Geschichte des deutschen Lehrervereins (Leipzig, 1908).

Wilke, E. Diesterweg und die Lehrerbildung (Berlin, 1890).

Schmid, K. A. Encyklopädie des gesamten Erziehungs- und Unterrichtswesen (Leipzig, 1887), Vol. X.

Administration

Baltzer, J. Die wichtigsten preussischen Schulordnungen der letzten drei Jahrhunderte.

Bremen, E. von. Die preussische Volksschule. Gesetze und Verordnungen (Berlin, 1905).
    Contains everything dealing with the administration of elementary and normal schools of Prussia.

Centralblatt für die gesamte Unterrichtsverwaltung (Berlin, monthly).
    The official organ of the Ministry in Prussia.

Commissioner of Education. Reports, U. S. Bureau of Education (Washington).

Englmann, J. A. und Stingl, E. Handbuch des bayerischen Volksschulrechts (Munich, 1905).

Handbuch für Lehrer und Lehrerinnen (Leipzig, 1903).
    A handbook for teachers dealing with administration of Prussian schools, the preparation of the teacher and the examinations, the legal status of teachers, teachers' associations and educational magazines.

Heinze, W. Im Amt (Goslar, 1906).
    Similar to the previous book.

HERBER, PAULINE. Das Lehrerinnenwesen in Deutschland (Munich, 1906).
Deals with the preparation and status of the women teachers.

GLATTFELTER, A. Das Lehrerbesoldungsgesetz vom 26 Mai, 1909 (Düsseldorf, 1909).
Contains the laws on salary, pension, and provision for widows.

KRETZSCHMAR, F. Handbuch des preussischen Schulrechts (Leipzig, 1899).
A clear account of the educational administration of Prussia.

KRETZSCHMAR, J. F. Das höhere Schulwesen im Königreich Sachsen, Gesetz vom 22 Aug., 1876 (Leipzig, 1903).

LEXIS, W. Das Unterrichtswesen im deutschen Reich (Berlin, 1904).
An excellent treatment of all phases of German education.

Pädagogisches Jahrbuch (Berlin, annually).
Gives a resumé of the administrative changes, the most important questions affecting elementary education and teachers, the transactions of teachers' associations, and reviews of books on education.

Pädagogische Jahresschau (Berlin, annually).
Similar to the previous book.

P··TZOLD, W. Geschichte des Volksschulwesens im Königreich Sachsen (Leipzig, 1908).

PLUSCHKE, P. Die städtischen Schuldeputationen und ihr Geschäftskreis (Berlin, 1908).
A very full account of the administration of education from the point of view of local boards of administration.

REIN, W. Encyclopædia.

Sächsische Landtagsakten (Dresden, annually).
The official statistical publication.

SCHÖPPA, C. Die Bestimmungen des königlichen preussischen Ministers, etc. (Leipzig, annually).
Contains the regulations for elementary, middle and normal schools, teachers' examinations, with the annual changes.

Statistisches Jahrbuch für den preussischen Staat (Berlin, annually).

SEYDEWITZ, P. VON. Das königliche sächsische Volksschulgesetz (Leipzig, 1906).

CURRICULUM

BREMEN, E. VON. See under administration.

ENGLMANN, J. A. und STINGL, E. See under administration.

GERSTENHAUER, O. Zur Würdigung der Lehrpläne von 1901 (Breslau, 1906).
A critical estimate of the course of study for normal schools.

GRÜLLICH, A. Unsere Seminar-Arbeit, Ein Beitrag zur Organisation des sächsischen Seminarwesens (Meissen, 1904).
An account of the curriculum in Saxon normal schools.

KRETZSCHMAR, J. F. See under administration.

LEXIS, W. Vol. III. See under administration.

SCHÖPPA, C. See under administration.

SCHMIDT, A. M. Über den gegenwärtigen Stand der Lehrerbildung und Lehrerinnenbildung in Thüringen. In Mitteilungen des Vereins der Freunde Herbartischer Pädagogik in Thüringen (Langensalza, 1907).
A comparison with the normal schools of Prussia.

Theory of Training Teachers

GERSTENHAUER, O.   See under curriculum.
GRÜLLICH, A.   See under curriculum.
Pädagogische Blätter.
    A magazine devoted entirely to this question.
SCHMIDT, A. M.   See under curriculum.
SEYFERT, R.   Vorschläge zur Reform der Lehrerbildung (Leipzig,   1905).
    A valuable contribution.

Teachers' Associations

Handbuch für Lehrer, etc.   See under administration.
Deutsche Lehrerverein, Berichte (Leipzig, annually).
    (The provincial associations publish annual reports.)
Deutsche Schule.
    The monthly organ of the Deutsche Lehrerverein.
Preussische Lehrerzeitung.   Weekly.
Leipziger Lehrerzeitung.
RISSMANN, R.   Geschichte des deutschen Lehrervereins (Leipzig, 1908).
    A history of teachers' associations, with a good account of the
    present position and activities of the Deutsche Lehrerverein.

Educational Museums

ANDREWS, B. R.   Museums of Education, their History and their Use,
    Teachers College Record, September, 1908.
HÜBNER, M.   Die deutschen Schulmuseen (Breslau, 1904).
    Das stadtische Schulmuseum zu Breslau (Breslau, 1902).
LEXIS, W.   See under administration.
MONROE, W. S.   Educational Museums and Libraries of Europe, *Educa-
    tional Review*, April, 1896.

For a list of educational magazines and current literature see Heinze,
W., Im Amt, p. 266 ff.

INDEX